More

FOX 13
TAMPA BAY

ONE TANK TRIPS®

with **BILL MURPHY**

Seaside
Publishing, Inc.

Publisher
Joyce LaFray

Design & Illustration
James Wahl
Kevin Coccaro

Editorial
Cary Williams
Kelli Kwiatkowski, Farrah Smolinski

Additional copies of this book may be ordered by calling:
1-888-ONE-TANK (663-8265)

Or you may write the Publisher at:

Seaside
Publishing, Inc.

P.O. Box 14441, St. Petersburg, FL 33733

Visit our Web site and order online at: **famousflorida.com**
E-mail: **sales@famousflorida.com**

ISBN: 0-942084-27-6

Library of Congress Catalog Number: 2001132940

Cover Photos — Front: Bill Murphy enjoys Chrysler's PT Cruiser in Safety Harbor,
at the Safety Harbor Resort & Spa (Trip #37). **Photo by Alex McKnight.**
Back: l. to r.: Church at St. Augustine (St. Johns County VCB);
Bill Murphy hits the road in the new Jeep Liberty (Photo by Alex McKnight);
Kayaking at Dragonfly Watersports (Photo by Steve Goldsmith); and
the Southernmost Point in Key West (Stuart Newman Associates).
Title page photos—top to bottom: Bill Murphy at Ft. DeSoto Park; (James Wahl/WTVT),
John's Pass (St. Pete/CW Convention Bureau); and Key West (Stuart Newman Associates).

Special Sales: Bulk purchases (12+ copies) of *FOX 13's More One Tank Trips With Bill Murphy*
are available to bookstores, gift shops, special groups, distributors, and wholesalers
at quantity discounts. For more information call: **1-888-ONE-TANK (663-8265)**, or write to:
Special Sales, Seaside Publishing, Inc., P.O. Box 14441, St. Petersburg, Florida 33733.

While we have been very careful to ensure the accuracy of the information in this guide,
time brings change and, consequently, the publisher cannot accept responsibility for errors
which may occur. All prices and opening times are based on information given to us
at press time. All prices are quoted without tax. Most trip directions are given with Tampa
as a starting point. **Admission fees and hours may change, so be sure to call ahead.**
Most trips have facilities for the handicapped, but do call ahead to confirm.
We welcome your comments and suggestions for future editions.

No maps, illustrations or other portions of this guide may be reproduced in
any form without written permission from the publisher.

Dedication

To my wife Karen and the girls for their support and love, and for enduring that alarm clock on early weekend mornings. And to my daughter, Jessica Leigh. With all my love.

Acknowledgments

Special recognition belongs to:

Robert Linger, Vice President & General Manager

Phil Metlin, News Director

Mike House, Creative Services Director

James Wahl, Design Director

Kevin Coccaro, Graphic Designer

Rick Hardman, Chief Photographer

Luke Marquis, Video Editor

Carrie Schroeder, Promotion/Publicity Manager

Nan Grable, Executive Assistant

And

Each and Every Member of the FOX13 Team

Also

Carolyn Forrest, Vice President, FTS

Chrysler and Jeep Dealers

FOX13 Switchboard Operators

The Staff at Seaside Publishing

contents

contents

Florida map

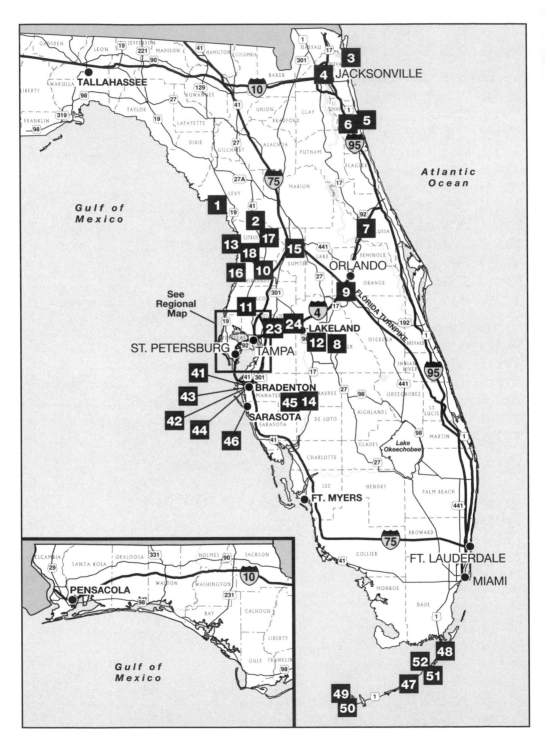

regional map

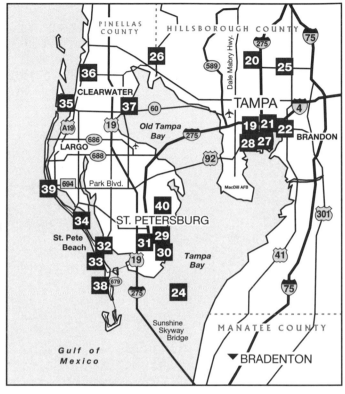

discover the **real** Florida

a word from FOX13

The overwhelming response to our first **One Tank Trips** book made a second inevitable. The first publication was the result of the many calls we received each time one of our **"One Tank Trip"** episodes aired. Our dedicated staff fielded numerous calls from viewers requesting information, directions, phone numbers and admission prices. The book answered all of those queries and more. And now *More* **One Tank Trips** satisfies the demand for even more excursions, highlighting 52 additional Florida destinations.

Our first book was published in November of 1999. Here then, two years in the making, is *More* **One Tank Trips.** Inside this guide are 52 new, unique Florida destinations that you can drive to on one tank of gas.

We hope you enjoy discovering these new adventures and attractions across our state as much as we have.

And, be sure to watch Bill Murphy on **FOX13** for your next **"One Tank Trip"!**

Robert W. Linger
Vice President & General Manager
WTVT FOX13 Television

Bill Murphy is a veteran TV news reporter and anchor who has spent more than 15 years in Tampa Bay broadcasting. He is the host of **FOX13**'s popular series of feature reports, **"One Tank Trips."** Bill spotlights one-of-a-kind destinations which take only one tank of gas or less to reach.

After moving to the Tampa Bay area in 1985, Bill became host of the popular talk show, "Murphy in the Morning," which received an Emmy nomination in 1991. Since then, Bill has been anchoring **"Good Day Tampa Bay"** on **FOX13,** the most successful morning newscast in Florida.

Before he came to Florida, Bill's broadcast career included seven years as anchor at KSBW-TV in Monterey, Calif., and stints in Seattle, Palm Springs and Los Angeles.

Bill has hosted the MDA and Easter Seal telethons and The Miss Florida Teen USA Pageant. He was named "Favorite Television Personality" and his show, "Murphy in the Morning," was voted "Best Local Talk Show" by *Tampa Bay Magazine.*

In November 1999, the launch of a new book, **One Tank Trips,** brought thousands of fans to over 100 autographing sessions at bookstores, gift shops, specialty stores, libraries and even Air Force bases.

When he's not watching the gas gauge and driving off on another intriguing **"One Tank Trip,"** Bill enjoys reading, tennis, handball, in-line skating and spending time with his wife Karen, his daughters and cats.

here we go again!

A few years back, while putting together our first **One Tank Trips**, I wondered, "Is this really a book people will want?" Now, as I write this introduction to *More* **One Tank Trips**, more than 100,000 copies of the first book have found their way into your homes, offices, and the glove compartments of cars, trucks and RVs. Add to that the countless phone calls, faxes, e-mails and letters I have received from many of you, and truly, you have made this one of the most memorable experiences in my life.

In your hand is *More* **One Tank Trips**, our new travel guide to fun in Florida. I know you will enjoy the trips in this book as much, if not more, than those in the first. It's my hope that you will enjoy these 52 new adventures as much as I have.

As I have always cautioned, call and confirm the details on each trip before you begin. Although we have checked again and again, things change. Also, be sure to check on the weather, always an important consideration while traveling.

My thanks to two guys with whom I worked closely on these 52 **"One Tank Trip"** adventures. One is "Sundance," the other, "The Luke of Earl." Sundance is **FOX13** Chief Photographer Rick Hardman, the fastest "shooter" in the East and probably the West. Video Editor Luke Marquis, a true child of the '60s (even though he wasn't around then), took Rick's videos and my words and pieced them together with great finesse.

Again, it's difficult for me to express how much I appreciate your warm words and compliments. Will there be a third? Stay tuned.

May all your travels be safe and, oh yes, happy trails to you!

Bill

ONE TANK TRIPS®

with BILL MURPHY

North Florida

The Village of Cedar Key

living on island time

Cedar Key Area Chamber of Commerce

Cedar Key Area Chamber of Commerce

The streets of downtown are lined with many historic homes, built with gables and porches, where residents preserve the island lifestyle.

the trip

Cedar Key is one of Florida's oldest ports and certainly one of the most beautiful. The peaceful setting reminds me of a time gone by. This lovely community has a unique appeal, attracting a multitude of artists and writers inspired by the pristine environment. The seafood you'll find here is abundant and superb!

what to see

Walk the historic streets, browse the shops and galleries, explore the back bayous and enjoy restaurants. One of the most popular is the Island Room Restaurant, which features fresh seafood from local waters. Have fun fishing, bird watching and hiking on nearby nature trails. Guides are also on call for off-shore trips to the outer islands. Many of these islands are part of the Cedar Key National Wildlife Refuge. Use the public marina for docking boats and other watercraft.

other highlights

Aquaculture is the cultivation of the waters' natural produce. It's a practice that flourishes here. Most of the luscious clams and oysters are now grown using new and faster methods. Thousands of visitors flock to Cedar Key for the annual Seafood Festival held in October, the Sidewalk Art Festival in April and the Fourth of July celebration.

Cedar Key Area Chamber of Commerce
480 Second Street
Cedar Key, FL 32625
(352) 543-5600

Admission: *Free*

Hours: *Restaurant and shop hours vary. Be sure to check ahead.*

www.cedarkey.com

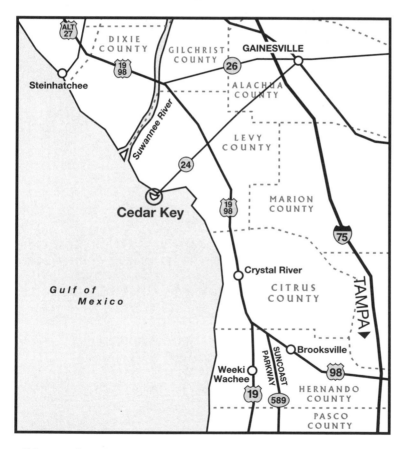

directions
From Tampa, take U.S. 19/98 north to S.R. 24, about 70 miles. Travel southwest on S.R. 24 about 20 miles to the village of Cedar Key. Cedar Key is 23 miles west of U.S. 19 at the end of S.R. 24.

" the 'key' to a fun day."

The Village of Cedar Key

Dragonfly Watersports

a great splash on the rivers

You are likely to see plenty of wildlife, like this cormorant, as you paddle your way down the Rainbow River.

Christopher Revis

Christopher Revis

the trip

Sherri and Steve Goldsmith are the mom-and-pop of Dragonfly Watersports. It's certainly an appropriate name in this neck of the woods, given the many delicate and gentle dragonflies found here. Rent a canoe, kayak or inflatable boat. Dragonfly Watersports is at your service.

what to see

Take your pick of the seven-mile-long, spring-fed Rainbow River, or the beautiful Withlacoochee River. They are both wonders to behold! What a perfect setting to simply sit back, paddle when you like...and enjoy. For non-swimmers, people with special needs, and parents with small children, inflatable boats are available as well

other highlights

If you're feeling a little more adventurous, Dragonfly Watersports offers longer trips to the Gulf barrier islands. Now, about those dragonflies: not only are they beautiful and amazing, their ancestors were around 100 million years before the dinosaurs! They are survivors, playing an important role in Florida's ecological chain. And despite their appearance, they do not sting and are quite harmless.

20336 E. Pennsylvania Avenue (Highway 484) Dunnellon, FL 34432 Toll free: (800) 919-9579 (352) 489-3046

Rates: *Kayaks: $30 (solo), $40 (double), $45 (triple). Canoes: $25 (solo), $30 (double), $35 (triple). Canoe and kayak rates are for a minimum two-hour trip. No extra charge for additional time. Inflatable boats: $15 (solo), $25 (double), $30 (triple). Approximate time for inflatable boat trips is three-and-one-half to four hours. Tubing: $8 per tube. Approximate time for tubing trip is four hours.*

Hours: *Check-in time for canoe and kayak rentals is 9 a.m. to 1:15 p.m. Check-in time for tubing and inflatable boat rentals is 9 a.m. to 11:15 a.m.*

www.dragonflywatersports.com

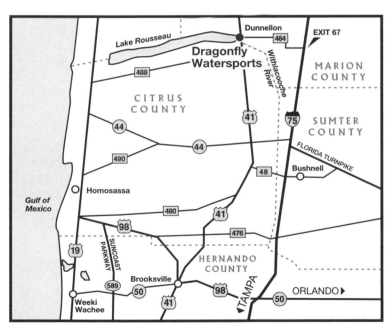

directions

From Tampa, take Interstate 75 north to Exit 67 (U.S. 484), just before Ocala. Go west (left) on U.S. 484 approximately 22 miles to Dunnellon. Dragonfly Watersports is on the left, about one-half mile after the Rainbow River Bridge over U.S. 484.

"spend an **hour** or a day **on** the water. It's **good** for what **ails** ya."

North Florida

Kingsley Plantation

preserving the past

Mike Booher

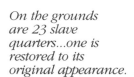

On the grounds are 23 slave quarters...one is restored to its original appearance.

Mike Booher

Zephaniah Kingsley and other plantation owners lived in this 1798 house.

the trip

Zephaniah Kingsley came to Spanish Florida in the early 19th century to make his fortune. He began by acquiring land and then building plantations using slaves to work the land. Kingsley Plantation (originally Fort George Island) was established in 1814. It represents a unique time and place in Florida history. The stories and contributions of a people, free and enslaved, can be explored in the many exhibits.

what to see

Visitors can tour Kingsley's residence, where he lived with his wife, Anna Madgigine Jai, and four children. Anna was a slave who Kingsley purchased and then freed. You will also see the ruins of what once were 23 tabby (oyster shell and concrete) cabins and learn about the cultivation of plantation crops. Fields of Sea Island cotton, the primary crop of the plantation, once covered much of the island.

other highlights

It's believed the plantation's main residence dates back to 1798. It's an unusual structure, with a two-story central area and four square corner rooms. Today, the visitor center and historical exhibits are located here.

11676 Palmetto Avenue Jacksonville, FL 32226 (904) 251-3537

Admission: *Free*

Hours: *Open daily 9 a.m. to 5 p.m. Closed Christmas Day.*

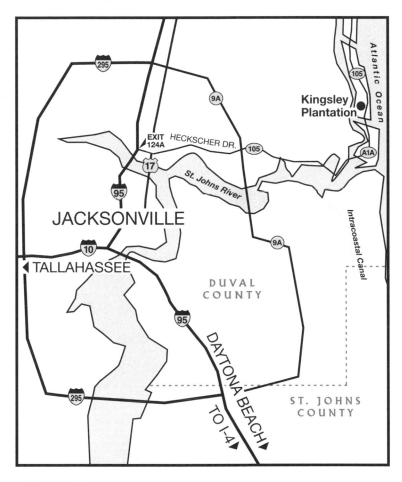

directions

From Tampa, take Interstate 4 north, merge onto Interstate 95 towards Jacksonville. Take Exit 124A (S.R. 105/Heckscher Drive) toward U.S. 17. Merge onto Heckscher Drive (which becomes A1A) and follow about 15 miles. Take a left onto Fort George Road, then another left onto Palmetto Avenue to Kingsley Plantation, about two miles.

"here at **Kingsley** Plantation the **stories** will be **told** forever."

Kingsley Plantation

The Ritz Theatre & LaVilla Museum

puttin' on the Ritz

An entire exhibit in the LaVilla Museum is dedicated to James Wheldon Johnson, a LaVilla native.

The Ritz Theatre and LaVilla Museum

The Ritz Theatre and LaVilla Museum

The restored Ritz Theatre is host to a variety of arts.

the trip

An old theater is new again! The famous Ritz Theatre, which opened in 1929, has been lovingly restored. The structure shines like it did when LaVilla, a Jacksonville neighborhood, earned the nickname "the Harlem of the South." Enjoy browsing through the 32,000-square-foot museum and theater. It features exhibits focusing on the history of African-American life in LaVilla and Northeast Florida.

what to see

The mission of the 11,000-square-foot museum is to discover, preserve, and share historical and cultural African-American experiences. The 400-seat theater plays host to weddings, national recording artists, touring productions and gospel shows. A must-see is the exhibit dedicated to James Weldon Johnson. The LaVilla native wrote the remarkable "Lift Every Voice and Sing." First a poem, then a song, it came to be known as the original African-American national anthem.

other highlights

The museum will tell you the complete story of LaVilla, the good and bad, the inspirational and regrettable. Experience the neighborhood drugstore the way it used to be, along with other historic section of the community. A part of the story is unique to Jacksonville, while another is a reflection of national changes.

826 N. Davis Street
Jacksonville, FL 32202
(904) 632-5555

Admission: *Museum: $4 adults, $2 students and seniors. Theater prices vary.*

Hours: *Open Tuesday through Friday 10 a.m. to 6 p.m., Saturday 10 a.m. to 2 p.m., Sunday 2 p.m. to 5 p.m. Theater hours vary.*

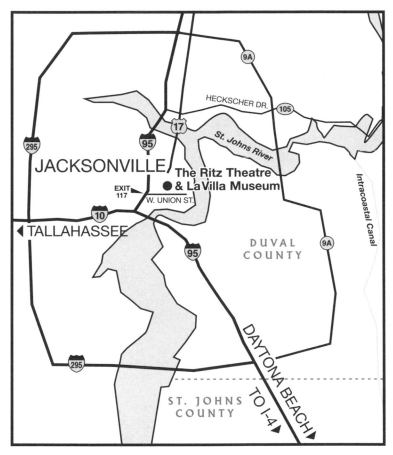

directions

From Interstate 4, merge onto Interstate 95 going north towards Jacksonville. Take Exit 117 (Union Street) towards the sports complex and riverfront. Merge onto West Union Street and follow about 400 feet to North Davis Street. Turn left and you will be at The Ritz Theatre and LaVilla Museum.

" once **known** as the '**Harlem** of the South,' there is a **wonderful** rebirth underway in **this** neighborhood."

North Florida

St. Augustine & The Castillo de San Marcos

history and "magic" at every turn

St. Johns County VCB

In St. Augustine, situated at the mouth of two rivers on the Atlantic, history endures at every turn.

St. Johns County VCB

the trip

Founded in 1565, St. Augustine is the oldest continuously occupied European settlement in the United States. The city is filled with much to see and do. Be ready to spend some time in this historic community.

what to see

You will want to bring your camera when you visit here! More than 80 historic sites and attractions await. A must-see is the romantic, historical Castillo de San Marcos on Matanzas Bay. It's the oldest masonry fort in the continental United States. Just to the south is the elegant Bridge of Lions. Nearby is historic St. George Street. It's the city's "outdoor mall," where you will find a collection of gift shops and restaurants. One of my most memorable stops is the Lightner Museum with its unusual furniture and a ballroom that was once the world's largest pool!

other highlights

Be sure to visit the Fountain of Youth. According to tradition, Ponce de Leon discovered this magical spring after he landed in St. Augustine on April 2, 1513. I bought 12 gallons!

St. Augustine Visitors Bureau
88 Ruberia Street, Suite 400
St. Augustine, FL 32084
(904) 829-1711

Castillo de San Marcos NM
One South Castillo Drive
St. Augustine, FL 32084

Admission: *St. Augustine, of course, is free. The Castillo de San Marcos is free to children 16 and under. Children must be accompanied by an adult. $4 for individuals, $50 for wedding permits.*

Hours: *Restaurant, shop, museum and attraction hours vary. Castillo is open 8:45 a.m. to 4:45 p.m. daily, except December 25th.*

www.visitoldcity.com

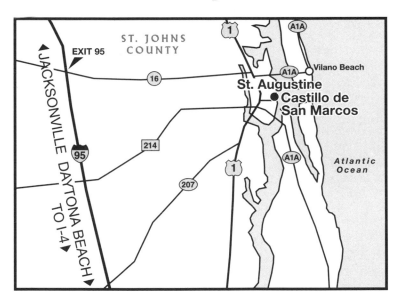

directions

From Tampa, take Interstate 4 north to Interstate 95. Take the St. Augustine Historic Sites and Downtown Exit (S.R. 16) to U.S. 1 (A1A). Head south on U.S. 1 for about two miles to One Castillo Drive. Parking is ahead on the left. Castillo de San Marcos is located in downtown St. Augustine.

" the sightseeing is nothing short of spectacular."

TRIP

6

North Florida

San Sebastian Winery

a wine for every taste

Children stomp grapes at the annual Harvest Festival.

the trip

Welcome to San Sebastian! Tucked away in a corner of historic St. Augustine, you will find the San Sebastian Winery. It's one of only a handful of wineries in all of Florida. This handsome structure is located on the San Sebastian inlet. It's part of a complex designed by Henry Flagler to house the historic East Coast Railway. These days, the focus is on the production of delicious wines. To date, more than 39 acres of hybrid bunch grapes have been planted in San Sebastian's 55-acre vineyard.

what to see

The barrel room of course! In the intimate setting you'll find wine for nearly every palate, including San Sebastian Reserva, Chablis, Vintners White and Red, Port, and Cream Sherry. The adventurous owners have entered many major competitions. Numerous awards are an indication of the success of their winemaking techniques, a talent that takes years to develop!

other highlights

Grape stomping competitions take place throughout the entire weekend of the winery's Harvest Festival celebration. There's also live music, tours, tasting and a special picnic area.

157 King Street
St. Augustine, FL 32084
Toll free: (888) 352-9463
(904) 826-1594

Admission: *Free*

Hours: *Individuals and groups are welcome Monday through Saturday 10 a.m. to 6 p.m., Sunday 11 a.m. to 6 p.m.*

www.sansebastianwinery.com

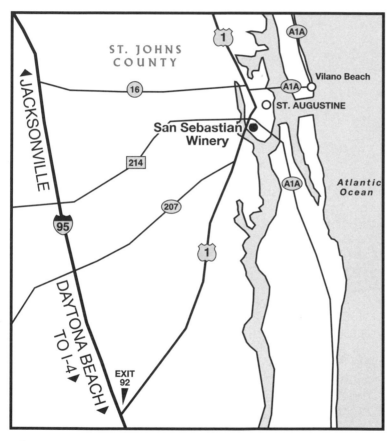

directions

From Tampa, take Interstate 4 east to Interstate 95. Go north (towards Jacksonville) on Interstate 95 to Exit 92 (U.S. 1/A1A) towards St. Augustine. Follow U.S. 1 about 16 miles, then turn right onto King Street. San Sebastian is about 100 yards down on your right.

Central Florida

Cassadaga Spiritualist Camp

communicating with spirit

Fran Ellison

The Andrew Jackson Davis Building sits at the entrance to the camp and houses the bookstore, pastors' office and Fellowship Hall.

Sunrise on Spirit Pond.

Fran Ellison

the trip

You will marvel at the quaint beauty of the 57-acre Cassadaga Spiritualist Camp. It's the oldest, active religious community in the Southeastern United States and was designated a Historic District on the National Register of Historic Places in 1991. The camp was founded by George P. Colby in 1894. Mr. Colby lived in New York, but he dreamed of a place in the South where his religion and spiritualism could be shared.

what to see

There are approximately 100 people who reside within the Cassadaga Spiritualist Camp. About half are practicing psychics or certified mediums available for readings and consultations. Residents may own their homes but the Camp retains ownership of the land. Sunday morning church services include hymns, a guided meditation, healing, a lecture, musical interludes and messages brought by a certified medium.

other highlights

It's important to distinguish between the town of Cassadaga and the Camp. Many businesses offer an array of religious and psychic readings, such as Tarot, palm divination and crystal ball gazing. Most are located around the perimeter of the Camp. The Camp does not invalidate these sciences when performed by experienced practitioners, but they are not carried out on camp grounds.

The Cassadaga Hotel & Psychic Center
355 Cassadaga Road
Cassadaga, FL 32706
(904) 228-2323

Admission: *Rates vary. Reservations are highly recommended.*

Hours: *Hours vary.*

www.cassadagahotel.com

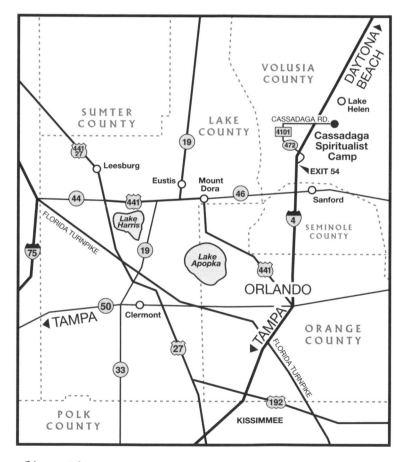

directions

From Tampa, take Interstate 4 north to Exit 54 (S.R. 472) towards Orange City/Deland. Follow the signs to Cassadaga, about four mile. (Cassadaga is 45 minutes northeast of Orlando and 15 minutes south of Deland).

"regardless **of** how you **feel** about psychics, Cassadaga **is** an **enchanting** destination."

Central Florida

Chalet Suzanne
Inn & Restaurant

an enchanting Old World tradition

Swiss-costumed waitresses pamper guests with the Chalet's famous Southern hospitality.

Chalet Suzanne

Chalet Suzanne

The Balcony Honeymoon guest room offers a luxurious, round bed and private dining balcony.

the trip

There is some wonderful magic going on at this European-style village. The Chalet's setting is lovely. It's surrounded by an orange grove in its own National Historic District. Four generations of the Hinshaw family have lived and worked at this 70-acre country inn. The Chalet's charming and talented owner, Vita Hinshaw, will welcome you as if you were family.

what to see

The Chalet has several gourmet dining rooms. A bridal suite overlooks one of them, with a dumbwaiter to deliver your meals. That way, you never have to leave…catch my drift? The Chalet's soup is world famous. As a matter of fact, it's out of this world — literally. This signature recipe, "Soup Romaine," is also called "Moon Soup." It was served up as a special freeze-dried delicacy to the crew of Apollo 16.

other highlights

Stop by the autograph garden. It's a beautiful setting and the site of many weddings. You can design your own "love" plaque at the ceramic shop and add it to others in the garden. There's also an antique shop, a gift shop, a library and a gourmet soup cannery, where the Chalet's famous soups are processed and then sold around the world. By the way, if you don't want to drive here, then fly. Chalet Suzanne has its own airstrip! Just let them know when you're coming.

3800 Chalet Suzanne Drive
Lake Wales, FL 33859
Toll free: (800) 433-6011
(863) 676-6011

Admission: *You are free to walk around the grounds and visit the restaurant and shops. Room rates vary from $169 to $229; special rates out of season. Room rates include a luscious English breakfast. Restaurant: Four-course lunches begin at $29, $14 for children under 12. A six-course candlelit dinner begins at $59. Children under 12 dine for $19.*

Hours: *Open year 'round.*

www.chaletsuzanne.com

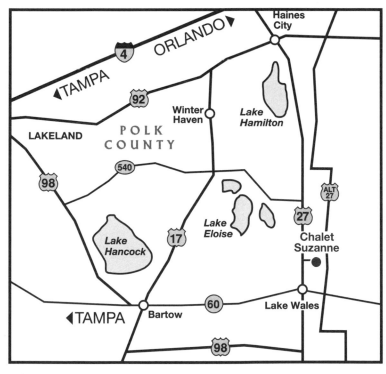

directions

From Tampa, take S.R. 60 east to Lake Wales. At Lake Wales take U.S. 27 north about four miles to Chalet Suzanne Road. Turn right and go east on Chalet Suzanne Road about one-and-three-quarter miles. The entrance is on the right.

"the **food** is **fabulous!**"

Gatorland

alligators abound

Oblivious to piggy-backing birds, thousands of gators enjoy their Gatorland home.

Gatorland

Gatorland

the trip

Set aside at least half a day to spend at this 110-acre park and wildlife preserve — long considered the "Alligator Capital of the World." It has one of the world's largest exhibits of giant gators. You'll also see free-flying lorikeets (Australian parrots), pink flamingos and a whole lot more!

what to see

The Gator Jumparoo show has made this attraction world-famous. You will be amazed as dozens of 13-foot gators leap out of the water and perform for their supper. And check out the gator wrestling, where the craziest of daredevils step into the ring to tangle with one of these fearless reptiles. It's man versus beast and quite a sight to behold!

other highlights

This place has thousands of gators, but trust me, there's something in the air here as well! Photographers from around the world journey to the 10-acre bird sanctuary. This refuge is home to many rare, endangered and protected species of birds. The preserve offers birdwatchers a unique opportunity to get up close and personal on an elevated walkway that winds through the alligator breeding marsh.

14501 S. Orange Blossom Trail
Kissimmee, FL 32837
Toll free: (800) 393-JAWS (5297)
(407) 855-5496

Admission: *$17.93 for adults, $8.48 for ages 3-12.*

Hours: *Open 9 a.m. to 6 p.m. daily. Closing times vary with the season.*

www.gatorland.com

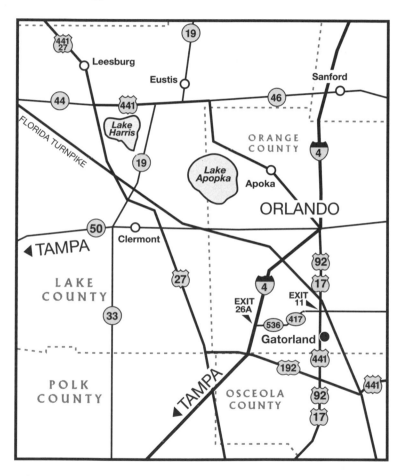

directions

From Tampa, take Interstate 4 east to Exit 26A (S.R. 536) which will become S.R. 417 N. Take Exit 11 onto U.S. 441 South, (Orange Blossom Trail), one mile south, and Gatorland will be on your left.

"see you **later...**"

Central Florida

9

Ho's Ponderosa Dude Ranch

experience the Old West in style

Throughout their stay, visitors learn the ins-and-outs of caring for their assigned equines.

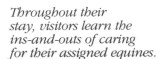

Ho's Ponderosa Dude Ranch

An authentic, Old West-style dude ranch, Ho's Ponderosa brings out the hidden cowboy in every city slicker.

Ho's Ponderosa Dude Ranch

the trip

This family-owned and operated Ponderosa is an authentic, full-service dude ranch. And whether your horseback ride is for an hour or a day, it won't take long for you to get into the Western spirit — even if you're a greenhorn like me!

what to see

Saddle up at the stable and take a ride through the scenic forest and over spectacular hills. Guests may saddle, groom and bathe their assigned horse throughout their stay, although it's not required. The bunkhouse is where you'll eventually rest your weary bones at day's end — great for cowboys and cowgirls of all ages.

other highlights

"Find Curley's Gold Weekend" is a ton of fun. Starting at 5 p.m. every Friday, each guest receives a copy of Curley's Map and is off on an adventure to find the "gold" by Sunday morning. At sundown, enjoy dinner and a singing cowboy by the campfire. You can also take a horse-drawn hayride, play volleyball, badminton, ping pong and croquet.

7586 S.W. 90th Avenue
Bushnell, FL 33513
Toll free: (877) 707-2624
(352) 793-2558

Admission: *Adults: $299 (2 nights, 3 days), $475 (4 nights, 5 days), $650 (6 nights, 7 days). Children 4-11: $175 (2 nights, 3 days), $325 (4 nights, 5 days), $425 (6 nights, 7 days). Children under 3: $25 (2 nights, 3 days), $50 (4 nights, 5 days), $75 (6 nights, 7 days). Includes: three meals per day, desserts, snacks, beverages (no alcohol served), horseback riding, hayrides, entertainment and all scheduled ranch activities.*

Hours: *Always open.*

www.hponderosa.com

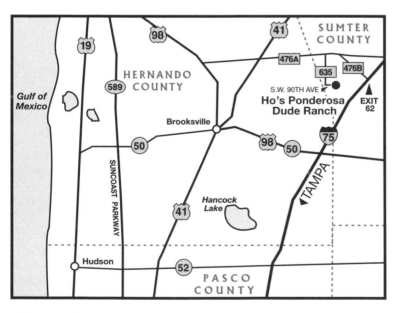

directions

From Tampa, take Interstate 75 north to Exit 62, turn onto C.R. 476B. Go four miles to the stop sign, then turn left at the stop sign to C.R. 476A. Go two miles to C.R. 635, turn left, then go three-quarters of a mile to the stop sign. Proceed straight onto a dirt road (approximately 500 ft.) to S.W. 90th Avenue. Take a left on S.W. 90th (approximately three-quarters of a mile) to Ponderosa Entrance on the left.

"saddle
up!"

Central Florida

J.B. Starkey's Flatwoods Adventures

real working ranch

These ranch residents love visitors; don't be surprised if you receive a cow kiss or two.

J.B. Starkey's

One look at J.B. Starkey's range buggy and you know this isn't your average school bus!

J.B. Starkey's

the trip

This thousand-acre ranch will take you back to Florida's unspoiled beauty of the late 1800s. Discover how J.B. Starkey, Sr. first realized his desire to become a cowboy and how he made his dreams of owning a cattle ranch come true.

what to see

Part of your adventure will be aboard the range buggy (a modified school bus). Learn all about ranch life and you may even see wild turkey, deer, boar and other wildlife on a fascinating two-hour eco-tour through the Starkey family ranch. A new 450-foot elevated boardwalk takes you through a cypress swamp for an up-close look at native plant life.

other highlights

If you care to saddle up like a real cowboy, the folks at Mac's Horse Riding Company will provide you with everything you need for a ride through 600 wild Florida acres. J.B. Starkey's also offers groups of 18 or more the opportunity to include a luncheon or dinner with their tour. The old-fashioned barbecue is the most popular. The picnic site is your call, either in the barn, or a mile back in the woods.

12959 State Road 54
Odessa, FL 33556
Toll free: (877) 734-9453

Admission: *$14.75 adults, $13.75 seniors, $7.75 children. Discounts for groups of 18 or more. Horseback Riding Tours: $60 per person (two-hour tour; no children under age 10 may ride).*

Hours: *Tour times vary; call for details. Reservations required for all tours.*

www.flatwoodsadventures.com

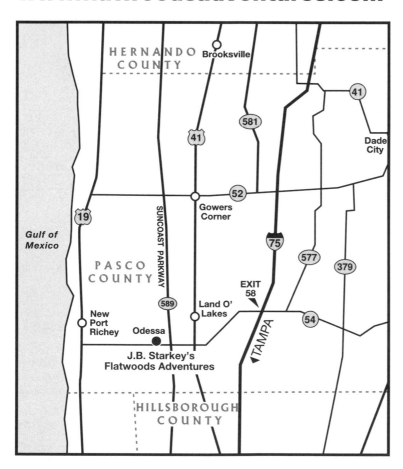

directions
From Tampa, take Interstate 75 north to Exit 58 (S.R. 54). Go west on S.R. 54. J. B. Starkey's is 18 miles down on the right.

"a flat-out **good** time."

Polk County Historical Museum

a valuable link to the past

The fascinating military exhibit is one of many inside the Polk County Historical Museum.

Polk County Historical Museum

Polk County Historical Museum

Extensive renovations have breathed new life into the Polk County Courthouse, including the beautiful Historical Museum rotunda.

the trip

The historic and newly renovated Polk County Courthouse in Bartow is impressive and really quite beautiful. Built in 1908, the courthouse is now home to the Polk County Historical Museum, where the standing invitation is "take a trip into the past."

what to see

You will find newspaper clippings, photos and fascinating information about old Polk County. If you're lucky, you'll run into Cotton Walker. He's a volunteer who has called Bartow home since the 1920's. This former world-class archer is also a contributor. Some of the antique bottles on display from his collection are more than 120 years old. And believe me, each bottle has a story. Walker also has an impressive collection of arrowheads, all found in Polk County. He found his first one on a camping trip with his son almost 35 years ago!

other highlights

On the second floor is a scale model of the Bethlehem Primitive Baptist Church in nearby Chikora. If you look closely, you will see holes in the floor under the two pews on the left. Cotton tells us these holes were for spittin' tobacco juice through!

100 E. Main Street
Bartow, FL 33830
(863) 534-4386

Admission: Free

Hours: Open Tuesday through Friday 9 a.m. to 5 p.m., Saturday 9 a.m. to 3 p.m.

www.polkcounty.net/library.html

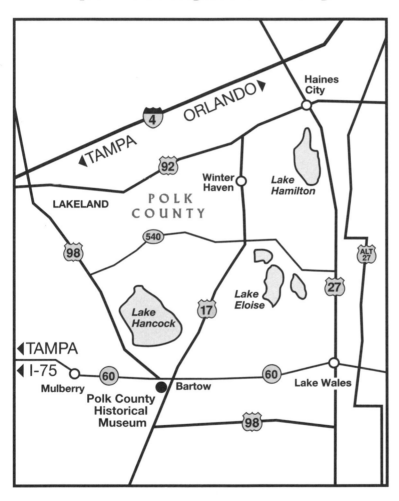

directions
From Tampa, head east on S.R. 60 for about 30 miles to Bartow. S.R. 60 turns into East Main Street in Bartow. The museum is near the intersection of Main Street and North Broadway.

"a true **slice** of Florida **history.**"

Central Florida

River Safaris & Gulf Charters

explore the beauty of the Nature Coast

River Safaris & Gulf Charters

Manatees welcome visitors during the winter months.

River Safaris & Gulf Charters

A tour down the lazy Homosassa River is a relaxing experience.

the trip

Many adventures await you at this mom-and-pop boat tour and rental facility on the beautiful Homosassa River. The owners, Captain Dennis Lowe and his wife Alicia, feel strongly about getting people out on the river to learn its history and to see this ballet of nature firsthand.

what to see

Ah, the river! There are several pontoon tours available. On the day we visited, we took a combination spring-and-backwater tour that meandered past Monkey Island, home to three spider monkeys — Ralph, Ebony and Sassy — and one squirrel monkey. You will also see a gazebo, once a favorite spot of President Grover Cleveland. The former Commander-In-Chief lived in Homosassa and could be seen fishing on warm, summer evenings. Be sure to spend a little time in the remarkable gallery and gift shop. It's a party for the eyes, with fun aquatic items everywhere.

other highlights

Another way to experience the tropical beauty of the Homosassa River is to jump right in! During the winter months you can swim with the manatees.

10823 Yulee Drive
Homosassa, FL 34448
Toll free: (800) 758-3474
(352) 628-5222

Rates: *Boat tours: From $15 per person for Spring and Backwater tours to $29 for the Long Backwater and Springs-to-Gulf trips. Boat rentals: From $15 for a one-hour canoe rental to $200 for a full-day, 29-foot pontoon rental.*

Hours: *8 a.m. to 5 p.m. daily. Tours depart at 9 a.m., 11 a.m., 1 p.m., 3 p.m., and 5 p.m.*

www.riversafaris.com

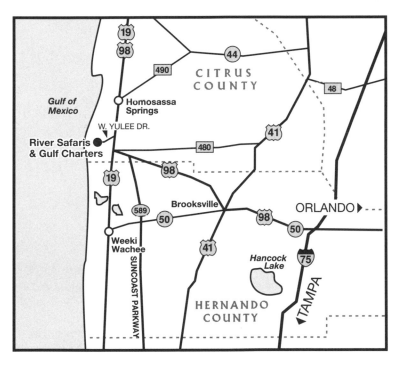

directions

From Tampa, take the Interstate 75 exit on U.S. 98 West towards Brooksville. Turn right (north) on U.S. 19 and proceed about 4-5 miles and make a left onto West Yulee Drive (currently a Burger King on the corner). Go two miles west on West Yulee Drive to the stop sign and turn left. River Safaris & Gulf Charters are located about one mile on the right.

"the **beauty** and serenity of **this** river will **soothe** your **soul.**"

Central Florida

Solomon's Castle

his home really is his castle!

Solomon's Castle

It's a pleasant surprise to find Solomon's Castle and The Boat in the Moat restaurant seemingly in the middle of nowhere.

Solomon's Castle

the trip

Three decades ago, an internationally known sculptor and host extraordinare settled near Ona and built a castle with his own hands. Be assured: If some people walk to the beat of a different drummer, then Howard Solomon has an entire symphony orchestra, with extra percussion!

what to see

There's lots of unique (to say the least) and amazing stuff to see here. The castle's exterior is big and shiny. It glistens and happens to be made from newspaper printing plates. Outside you will see a tower and more than 80 interpretive stained glass windows. Inside are extensive galleries, a stained-glass production studio and the family's living quarters. And there's "The Blue Room," a spacious suite available for overnight or weekend stays.

other highlights

While out in this middle-of-nowhere location, take advantage of the miles of beautiful nature trails around picturesque Horse Creek.

4533 Solomon Road
Ona, FL 33865
(863) 494-6077

Admission: *$7.50 adults, $3 children.*

Hours: *Open Tuesday through Sunday 11 a.m. to 4 p.m. Closed July, August and September.*

www.solomonscastle.com

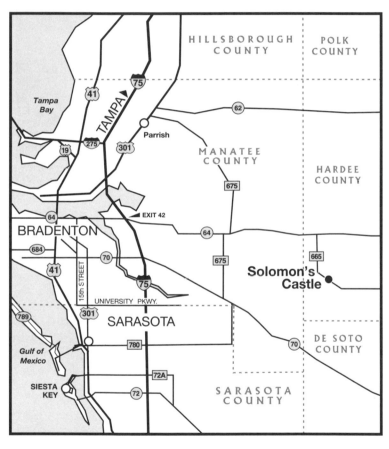

directions

From Interstate 75 South, take Exit 42 (S.R. 64, Bradenton/Wauchula/Zolfo Springs). Turn left on S.R. 64 and go east about 30 miles to C.R. 665. Turn right on C.R. 665 and go south for about nine miles. Take a hard left on C.R. 665 and go north for 140 feet. Bear right on Solomon Road and follow less than a mile to Solomon's Castle.

" with Howard **Solomon,** the one-liners and **smiles** are **a** dime a **dozen.**"

Solomon's Castle

Central Florida

Webster Flea Markets

Florida's attic

Webster Westside Flea Market

There is a lot of activity and plenty of goodies to choose from every Monday, flea market day in Webster.

Webster Westside Flea Market

the trip

Ready to do some serious shopping? Well, do we have some flea markets for you! The Webster Westside Flea Market is the largest and oldest flea market in Florida. Add in the Sumter County Farmer's Market across the street along with two smaller markets and you'll have quite a day!

what to see

Here you will find an absolutely remarkable and enormous mix of people and stuff — LOTS of stuff and LOTS of people — but only on Mondays. The Monday thing started during the Depression. Local farmers, facing tough times, organized a farmers co-op. The "blue law" kept them from doing business on Sundays. So hello Monday! On some days, there are as many as 4,000 dealers and 100,000 shoppers. That's a LOT!

other highlights

There are several flea markets in Webster. The Sumter County Farmer's Market, across from Webster Westside, is one of the largest. This market attracts about 1,200 dealers in the summer and 2,000 during the winter. It features antiques, jewelry, furniture, fresh produce, plants, citrus trees and more. As for food, there are plenty of concession stands everywhere. Don't forget to pick up two bags of Kettlecorn (one for me ... thank you very much).

Webster Westside Flea Market
516 N.W. Third Street
Webster, FL 33597
Toll free: (800) 832-3477
(352) 793-9877

Sumter County Farmer's Market
524 W. Market Boulevard
Highway 471
Webster, FL 33597
(352) 793-2021

Admission: *Free. Parking costs about $3.*

Hours: *Open every Monday 6 a.m. to 3 p.m.*

www.websterfleamarket.com

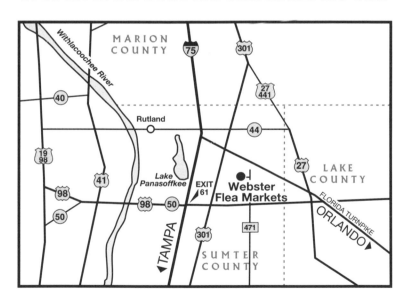

directions

From Tampa, take Interstate 75 north to Exit 61 (Orlando/ Brooksville). Keep left at the fork in the ramp, then turn right onto U.S. 98/S.R. 50 East. Turn left onto S.R. 50, go north about 10 miles, then take a left (north) onto S.R. 471 (which becomes North Market Blvd.). From S.R. 471 turn onto Northwest Fourth Avenue. Follow the signs to the Webster Flea Markets, less than a mile down the road.

" this
One Tank Trip
is really
a trip!"

Central Florida

Weeki Wachee Canoe Rental

paddle your troubles away

The natural beauty of the river
surrounds you at Rogers Park.

Weeki Wachee Canoe Rental

Whether you wade in or swing
from a rope Tarzan-style, be sure
to take advantage of the crystal
clear Weeki Wachee waters.

Weeki Wachee Canoe Rental

the trip

Encounter the beauty of the crystal clear Weeki Wachee River from a canoe or kayak. Normally, the current is not strong and paddling is fairly easy. When you reach the end of your eight-mile journey at Rogers Park, transportation will be waiting for the short drive back to where you began.

what to see

Along the trip, expect to see plenty of wildlife, including manatees, turtles and birds. Once you are past the large "Wildlife Preserve" sign (about 20-30 minutes from the ramp) you can also go swimming or fishing. There's also a nice little beach with a sandy bluff behind it, about four miles into your expedition — a great spot to take a little siesta.

other highlights

Have a good ghost story, or perhaps there's a loved one you'd like to serenade? Ask about the moonlight canoe trips. After your visit, spend some time at the Weeki Wachee Springs Waterpark. It's one of Florida's oldest theme parks and home to those famous, beautiful mermaids. Weeki Wachee was featured in our first **"One Tank Trips"** book.

6131 Commercial Way
Spring Hill, FL 34606
(352) 597-0360

Admission: *$31 per two-seat canoe; $22 per single-seat kayak. Includes seat backs, life jackets, paddles and the ride back upstream.*

Hours: *Last launch is at 1 p.m. Last pick-up is at 5 p.m.*

www.floridacanoe.com

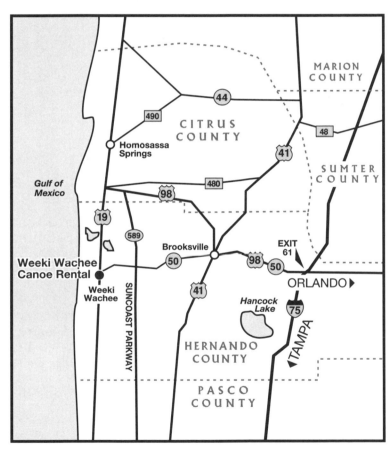

directions
From Tampa, take Interstate 75 north to Exit 61 (S.R. 50/ U.S. 98 West) west about 20 miles to U.S. 19. Weeki Wachee Canoe Rental is next door to the Weeki Wachee Springs Waterpark at the intersection of U.S. 19 and S.R. 50/U.S. 98.

"It **takes** about two seconds **to realize** this is going to **be** a **wonderful** ride."

Central Florida

Withlacoochee State Trail

nature-lovers utopia

The trail's smooth, paved roads — combined with good company — make for a fun, healthy excursion.

Judith Watson

Visitors will marvel over the Withlacoochee State Forest, featuring some of the most beautiful scenery in Florida.

Judith Watson

the trip

The trail is a paved 46-mile long, 12-foot wide stretch of old railroad bed that's been converted into a recreational area. The World Wildlife Fund calls it one of the "10 Coolest Places in North America." It's great for cycling, hiking and horseback riding.

what to see

From one end of Citrus County to the other, the trail meanders through some of the wildest, most beautiful scenery in all of Florida. Much of the trail passes through the Withlacoochee State Forest. It is the second largest state forest in Florida, covering more than 154,000 acres. There are several waterways and many varieties of trees. All combine to create dense woodlands and canopy trails. An abundance of colorful wildflowers excite the senses, especially in the spring.

other highlights

A portion of the trail includes Fort Cooper, a temporary fortification established in 1836 during the Second Seminole War. At certain times of the year, mainly in the fall and winter, the forest surrounding the trail becomes a hunting area. Fishing is also a popular activity on the Withlacoochee waterways. Panfish and largemouth bass are frequently caught here. And you know, there's nothing like taking home a good fish story (especially about the one that got away)!

Withlacoochee State Trail & Fort Cooper
3100 South Old Floral City Road Inverness, FL 34450 (352) 726-0315

Admission: *Free. $2 per carload for Fort Cooper.*

Hours: *Open 365 days a year, 8 a.m. to sundown.*

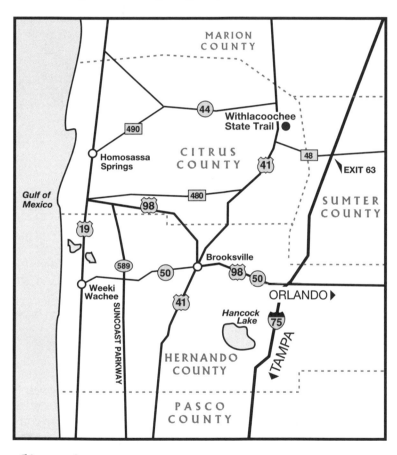

directions

From Tampa, take Interstate 75 to Exit 63 (Bushnell Exit/ S.R. 48). Turn left (west) on S.R. 48 and follow to the first traffic light (U.S. 41). Turn right onto U.S. 41 (go north) to the next traffic light (a few miles up the road) to Eden Drive. Turn right. Go to the first stop sign light (Old Floral City Road). Fort Cooper State Park and the Withlacoochee State Trail (you just crossed) are about a mile to your right.

"miles and **miles** of happy **trails!**"

Chassahowitzka River Tours

eco-tourism at its best

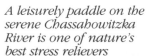

A leisurely paddle on the serene Chassahowitzka River is one of nature's best stress relievers

Ken Luther

Ken Luther

A bird-lover's delight, Chassahowitzka is home to herons, grackles and a wide variety of other birds.

the trip

Just south of Homosassa lies a serene and tranquil slice of true Florida beauty: the Chassahowitzka ("Chas-ah-hoe-wit-ska") River. In the Seminole Indian language, Chassahowitzka means "place of hanging pumpkin." It is a feast for the eyes in any language. Captain Ken Luther, owner of Chassahowitzka River Tours, is a wealth of information when it comes to the area. He shares that knowledge freely and with great joy during his pontoon tours.

what to see

The Chassahowitzka National Wildlife Refuge covers more than 30,000 acres. The trip begins in the river's spring-fed fresh water. The shore is dotted with cypress, oaks, cedars, sweet gum and a variety of other trees. With the salty waters of the Gulf of Mexico ahead, you may catch sight of deer, black bears, raccoons or perhaps a bobcat. During my travels on the river, I was even treated to the magnificent site of a bald eagle!

other highlights

The river is home to many fish, dolphins, gators and even manatee (I saw three on my trip!). Bird-lovers should bring binoculars for a glimpse of Louisiana herons, yellow-crowned night herons, boat-tailed grackles and other feathered friends. Bring sunscreen and hats, along with a picnic lunch to enjoy during your quick stop on "Dog Island."

10203 S. Zaneri Circle
Homosassa, FL 34448
(352) 382-0837

Admission: *One hour: $10 per person ($30 minimum); two hours: $15 per person ($35 minimum); three hours: $20 per person ($40 minimum). Children under 12 pay half price; free for ages 5 and under.*

Hours: *Tours are offered daily at 10 a.m. and 1 p.m. Special arrangements can be made for alternate times.*

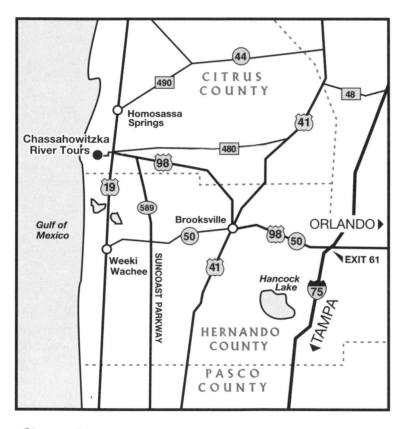

directions

From Tampa, take Interstate 75 north to Exit 61 (U.S. 98/ S.R. 50). Stay on S.R. 98 through Brooksville until you get to U.S. 19. Continue straight through the blinking light which becomes Miss Maggie Drive. Follow the yellow line in the middle of the road until it ends (1 mile). Turn right into the campground and continue another 1/4 mile which dead ends at the boat ramp.

"this **is** a **day** you'll **remember.**"

TRIP
19

The African Art Gallery & Museum

a Tampa treasure

Hillsborough County – West Central Florida

An ancient wood-carved chest from West Africa.

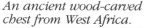

The African American Art Gallery and Museum

The African American Art Gallery and Museum

Paintings by Highwayman artist Mary Ann Carroll, "Sea Escape" and the "Royal Poinciana Tree." The statues are "Thinkers" from Senegal, West Africa.

the trip

The 4,400-square-foot gallery and museum near downtown Tampa houses authentic African art from various time periods. Local, national, and international artists contribute to this unique collection of artwork.

what to see

The craftsmanship of the pieces in The Benya Collection (meaning "Never to be Found") is fascinating. Many of the ancient artifacts and masterpieces, representing various African tribes, are heirlooms that have been passed down through generations. Fine examples include wood carvings, musical instruments, baskets, masks and statues. One of the prized collections, an ancient warrior's vest and shield designed by the great Zulu chief, Shaka, dates back to the 1700s.

other highlights

While the museum pieces are for display only, you can purchase wall hangings, modern furnishings and other items from the gallery.

1711 W. Kennedy Boulevard
Tampa, FL 33606
(813) 258-0223

Admission: *Gallery admission is free. Museum tours cost $5 for adults, $3 for children.*

Hours: *Open Wednesday through Friday 4:30 p.m. to 6 p.m., Saturday 11 a.m. to 6 p.m.*

www.africanart4sale.com

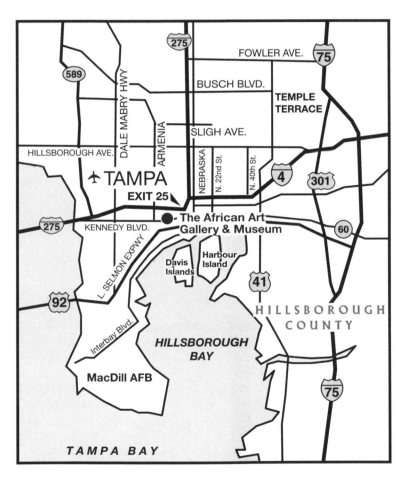

directions

From Tampa, take Interstate 275 to Exit 25 (Downtown/West). Merge onto North Ashley Drive. Turn right on Kennedy Boulevard and follow to the African Art Gallery and Museum on your right.

"this place **is** remarkable... **I** marveled at the **collection.**"

The African Art Gallery and Museum

Hillsborough County – West Central Florida

Buccaneer Heaven

get your gear here!

Buccaneer Heaven

Buccaneer Heaven

Bucs fans shop 'til they drop at Tampa's Buccaneer Heaven.

the trip

You bet it's heaven! Whether you're a casual fan, or a dyed-in-the-wool, no-hope-for-recovery Bucs fanatic, this place is amazing! It is one of the largest Bucs merchandise stores around. The shop was once named "Authentic Team Merchandise." But so many Bucs fans were overheard saying "this place is heaven," owners Jeff and Sara Ann Fox took the ball and ran with it!

what to see

Thousands of Bucs items fill more than 4,000 square feet of space. This place has it all, from jackets to shirts, baseball caps and shorts, to stuffed animals, flags, banners and those fuzzy footballs.

other highlights

Want to look like a bona fide Buc, or show your support for particular team members? While visiting this red and pewter palace, be sure to pick up an official Bucs jersey with the name of your favorite player.

14823 N. Florida Avenue
Tampa, FL 33613
Toll free: (800) 881-BUCS (2827)
(813) 908-2827

Admission: *Free. Prices of items vary.*

Hours: *Off-season: Monday through Saturday 10 a.m. to 6 p.m. Football Season: Monday through Saturday 10 a.m. to 7 p.m. Call for Sunday hours during football season.*

http://store.rivalgear.com/
abautteammer.html

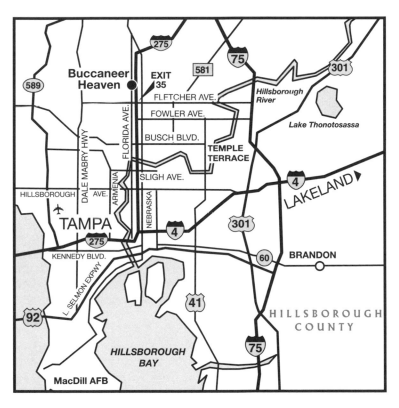

directions

From Tampa, take Interstate 275 north to Exit 35 (Fletcher Avenue). Turn left on Fletcher Avenue and head west. Turn right (north) on North Florida Avenue and travel about a half-mile to Buccaneer Heaven on the right. Parking is in front of the store.

"Bucs fans stop here!"

Hillsborough County – West Central Florida

Ybor City State Museum

one man's vision

Ybor City State Museum

Seventh Avenue, old Ybor City.

Firefighters relax in front of Ybor casitas after a hard day's work.

Ybor City State Museum

the trip

Experience the rich and colorful history of a society built around cigars inside the remarkable Ybor City State Museum. Don Vicente Martinez Ybor was born in Valencia, Spain in 1818. He spent many years in Cuba and Key West before coming to Tampa when he opened Ybor's first cigar factory in 1886. He is considered Tampa's first industrial baron.

what to see

The museum chronicles the story of Ybor and the diverse group of people who came here to live and work. A pleasant walking tour takes you to a *casita*, or little house. These early homes of cigar workers are called "shotgun houses" because of their long, narrow frames. In the late 1800s, they rented for $2.50 per week and sold for anywhere between $400 and $900.

other highlights

Outside, the gardens have been the site of many weddings and other special events. Find a souvenir in the unique little gift shop, including, of course, fresh hand-rolled cigars!

1818 Ninth Avenue
Tampa, FL 33605
(813) 247-6323

Admission: *$2 per person.*

Hours: *Open 9 a.m. to 5 p.m. daily.*

www.ybormuseum.org

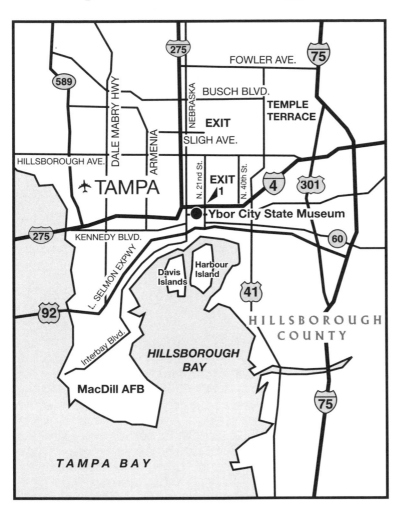

directions
From Tampa, take Interstate 4 to Exit 1 (21st Street) south to Palm Avenue. Turn right on Palm Avenue, then left on 19th Street. Turn right onto Ninth Avenue. The Ybor City Museum is less than a block up on the right.

"Tampa's **cultural** connection."

The Columbia Restaurant

100 years and going strong

The Patio Room is one of the Columbia's 11 dining areas.

The Columbia Restaurant

Frank Atura

The Columbia's famous flamenco dancers.

the trip

It opened in 1905 as a small corner café and was frequented by local cigar workers. Today, the original Columbia Restaurant is in its fourth and fifth generation of family ownership. Founded by Cuban immigrant Casimiro Hernandez, Sr., it is Florida's oldest and largest Spanish restaurant. Some of the world's best known celebrities, athletes, entertainers and politicians have dined and danced at The Columbia.

what to see

The original restaurant in Ybor City seats more than 1,600 persons in 11 spacious dining rooms. The Gonzmart family, led by Casey and Richard Gonzmart, serves thousands of traditional Spanish and Cuban meals every day of the week. Paella à la Valenciana, Red Snapper Alicanté and Trout a la Rusa are just a few of the excellent entreés that bring back locals again and again. Check out the Spanish Flamenco Dancers, considered the best in all of Florida. The décor, which includes hundreds of hand-painted tiles depicting the fanciful world of Don Quixote, is simply astounding.

other highlights

Enjoy live jazz, tapas, spirits and, of course, the finest cigars at The Cigar Bar Café. It's been called "America's Original Cigar Bar" by *Cigar Aficionado Magazine*. You can also visit one of five additional Columbia Restaurants, all a "One Tank" from the Tampa Bay area, in Clearwater Beach, Celebration, Sarasota, St. Augustine and St. Petersburg.

2117 E. Seventh Avenue
Tampa, FL 33605
(813) 248-4961

Admission: *Free. Prices of menu items vary. See Web site for menu.*

Hours: *Open daily 11 a.m. to 9:30 p.m. Open Friday and Saturday until 10 p.m.*

www.columbiarestaurant.com

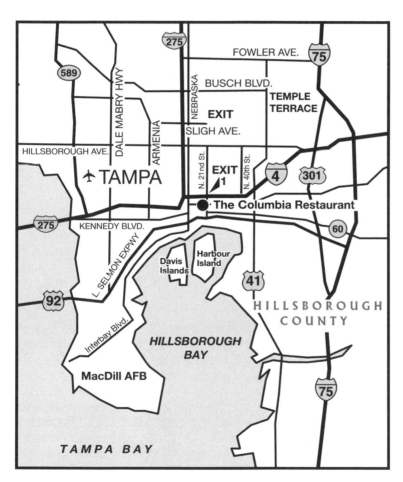

directions

From Tampa, take Interstate 4 to Exit 1 (21st Street) south to East Seventh Avenue. The Columbia Restaurant is at the corner of East Seventh Avenue and 21st Street. Parking is to the rear.

"chat over a café con leché."

Dinosaur World

giants of the past

Dinosaur World

Dinosaur World

The Tyrannosaurus Rex (above) and the Protoceratops, two of 150 dinosaurs in Dinosaur World.

the trip

This former alligator farm has been transformed into the world's largest dinosaur attraction. The setting is a subtropical jungle, with dinosaurs around virtually every corner. This is a place for kids of all ages.

what to see

At this 12-acre outdoor museum you will walk among more than 150 life-size models of dinosaurs that roamed the earth during the Permian, Triassic, Cretaceous and Jurassic periods. You'll see Stegosaurus, Protoceratops, Tyrannosaurus Rex and many more! These remarkable fiberglass dinosaurs are made in Sweden.

other highlights

There are plenty of hands-on activities, such as fossil digs for the kids and a large playground which recently opened. If you like, bring a picnic lunch and enjoy the cool shade of cypress, maple, gum and bay trees. And don't forget to pick up a unique souvenir from the gift shop.

5145 Harvey Tew Road
Plant City, FL 33565
(813) 717-9865

Admission: *$9.75 adults, $8.95 seniors over sixty, $7.75 children 3-12, free for children under 3. Free parking.*

Hours: *Open 365 days from 9 a.m. to dusk.*

www.dinoworld.net

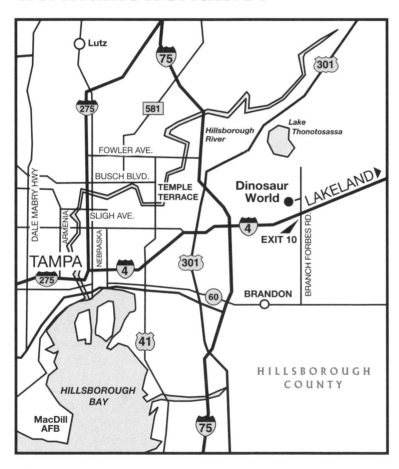

directions

From Tampa, take Interstate 275 North to Interstate 4. Take Exit 10 (Branch Forbes Road) turn left (north). Go under Interstate 4, then turn left almost immediately onto Harvey Tew Road. Go about 1500 feet and turn into the Dinosaur World parking lot.

"believe me, **these** are not lounge **lizards!"**

Historic Plant City

more than just strawberries

You can still get a Cherry Smash for a nickel at the Whistle Stop Café.

Michelle Newsome

Union Station Welcome Center

The former train depot has been converted into the Downtown Welcome Center.

the trip

When you think of Plant City, chances are you think of the annual Florida Strawberry Festival. And what a delicious event it is! But there's much more. Named for railroad tycoon Henry Bradley Plant, historic Plant City has undergone a major restoration in recent years and downtown is the place to be.

what to see

Begin your tour at the Union Station Welcome Center on Palmer Street, which many years ago was the train depot. Today you can relive those famous railroad days at the Historic Train Depot and Museum. Pick up a downtown walking map to use as a guide. Take a stroll and explore the many shops and eateries in this neck of the woods. At the Whistle Stop Café, order a Cherry Smash for the old-fashioned price of a nickel! Oh, and don't forget about the Strawberry Festival, always held in late February or early March.

other highlights

Talk a leisurely walk and glimpse into Plant City's fascinating past. Visit the 1914 high school and the many antique, collectible, and specialty shops along the historic brick streets. Within these renovated buildings, you'll find Aunt Nellie's, Miss Vicki's and Miss Emma's. Other shops of interest are Yesterdays Attic, Antiques and More, Heritage and Wallace's.

Hillsborough County – West Central Florida

The Greater Plant City Chamber of Commerce
106 N. Evers Street
Plant City, FL 33565
Toll free: (800) 760-2315
(813) 754-3707

Admission: *Free*

Hours: *Shop and restaurant hours vary. Call ahead for details.*

www.plantcity.org
info@plantcity.org

"there's **more** to this **charming** community **than** that **famous** berry."

directions

From Tampa, take Interstate 4 and head east to Exit 11 (Thonotosassa Road). Turn east on Thonotosassa Road, then follow it for about one mile to East Reynolds Street. Bear left on East Reynolds Street and follow it less than a mile into Historic Plant City.

Museum of Science & Industry (MOSI)

blinding you with science

Hillsborough County – West Central Florida

TRIP 25

Guests are blown away by MOSI's Gulf Coast Hurricane simulator.

Scott Martin

The Boeing 747-100 cockpit is a favorite among would-be pilots.

Scott Martin

the trip
The Museum of Science & Industry (MOSI) occupies 245,000 square feet on 65 acres in North Tampa. It's the largest science center in the Southeastern United States. It's also home to one of only two IMAX® Dome theaters in Florida, the world's largest and most powerful motion picture format.

what to see
You'll have to look real hard to find any "please do not touch" signs. Touching is not only allowed, it's encouraged! This is an interactive environment, with more than 450 hands-on activities for everyone. Try your hand at flight at "Our Place in the Universe." A far more gentle and beautiful kind of flight can be found at the BioWorks Butterfly Garden, where the aerial ballet is nonstop! You can literally get blown away in the Gulf Coast Hurricane exhibit. And take some time to explore our galaxy at The Saunders Planetarium.

other highlights
Visit MOSI's science store and take home your own science experiment. They also carry games, gifts, gadgets, videos, CDs, books and more.

More One Tank Trips

4801 E. Fowler Avenue
Tampa, FL 33617
Toll free: (800) 995-6674
(813) 987-6300

Admission: *$13 adults, $11 ages 50 and older, $9 ages 2-13, free for children under 2.*

Hours: *Open daily 9 a.m. to 5 p.m.*

www.mosi.org

directions
From Tampa, take Interstate 275 north to Exit 54 East (Fowler Avenue/S.R. 582A) then continue east for just over three miles. Turn right into MOSI.

" more than a day's worth of fun stuff to do."

Tampa Bay Downs
Horse Racing Track

get your heart racing

About the only thing better than a day at the races is a winning day at the races.

Tom Cooley

A field of horses turning for the homestretch.

Tom Cooley

the trip

Whether you come to place a bet or just enjoy the day, the 75-year-old Tampa Bay Downs Horse Racing Track is full of surprises.

what to see

The horses, of course! See and wager on both live and simulcast races nearly every day of the year from the grandstand, clubhouse or veranda. Live racing takes place on a newly installed Turf Course, offering distances of one-and-a-sixteenth and one-and-an-eighth miles.

other highlights

Whether you're betting or just here for fun, check out the races in style! Groups can reserve an exclusive Party Suite. Situated on the third floor, the private room features climate-controlled comfort, an exciting view of the finish line and great food. In the paddock area you can get super close to the action! You can almost reach out and touch these beautiful horses as they are saddled and the jockeys mount up.

11225 Race Track Road
Oldsmar, FL 34077
Toll free: (800) 200-4434
(813) 855-4401

Admission: *$2 general admission, $3 clubhouse. General parking is free, $2 preferred parking. Restaurant, bar and group rates vary.*

Hours: *Gates open 11 a.m. daily. Closed Christmas.*

www.tampabaydowns.com

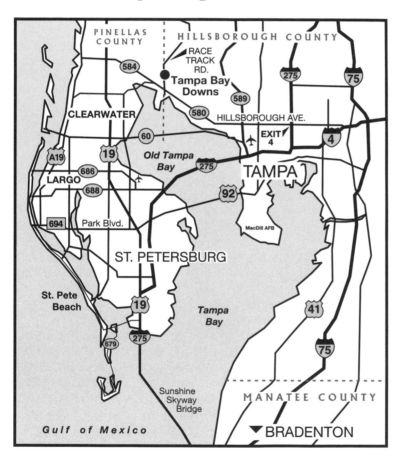

directions

From Tampa, go north to Exit 4 (Hillsborough Avenue West), then head west on S.R. 580 to Race Track Road. Turn right; less than a mile down Race Track Road you will see Tampa Bay Downs.

"my bet is you'll have a fun day!"

Tampa Bay Downs Horse Racing Track

Tampa Museum of Art

be one of the 80,000 visitors a year

Hillsborough County – West Central Florida

Even the entrance to the Tampa Museum of Art is a lesson in art appreciation.

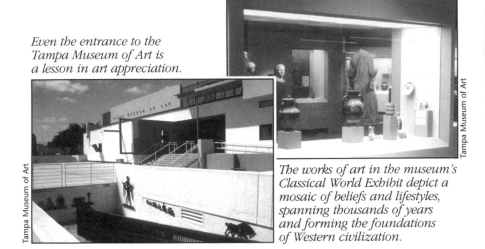

Tampa Museum of Art

Tampa Museum of Art

The works of art in the museum's Classical World Exhibit depict a mosaic of beliefs and lifestyles, spanning thousands of years and forming the foundations of Western civilization.

the trip

Each visit to this incredible museum is different from the one before. Along with ever-changing exhibitions, the museum's large inventory is rotated frequently. The focus is 20th century and contemporary art. You'll also be treated to one of the finest classical antiquities galleries in the Southeast. And there's much more: lectures, seminars, walking tours and children's activities. Take a moment to enjoy the picturesque back drop of the scenic Hillsborough River and the gleaming minarets of the University of Tampa.

what to see

With more than 400 objects on display, the antiquities exhibition illustrates artwork characteristic of ancient Greece and Rome. One piece, I noticed, is dated to 300 B.C. The collection is simply amazing! You'll find sculptures in bronze, marble, terra cotta, as well as struck silver and gold coins, ancient glass vessels and magnificent painted pottery. While you're here, take in the work of C. Paul Jennewein, a noted classical and art deco sculptor who visited the Bay area often.

other highlights

Your visit won't be complete without a stop at the museum store. Far more than just a gift shop, you will find many unique items, including a fabulous collection of one-of-a-kind jewelry. Take a tour of the charming grounds of the University of Tampa, then finish with a delicious Florida-style meal at Mise en Place, located nearby on West Kennedy Boulevard.

600 N. Ashley Drive
Tampa, FL 33602
(813) 274-8130

Admission: *$5 adults, $4 ages 62 and older, $3 ages 6 to 18 and students, free for children under 6. Admission is free Saturday 10 a.m. to noon and Thursday 5 p.m. to 8 p.m.*

Hours: *Open Tuesday through Saturday 10 a.m. to 5 p.m., Thursday 10 a.m. to 8 p.m., Sunday 1 p.m. to 5 p.m. The museum store is also open Monday 10 a.m. to 5 p.m.*

www.tampamuseum.com

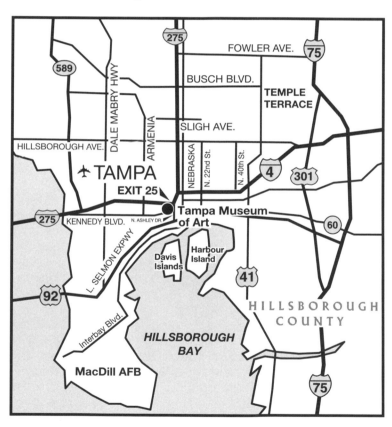

directions

From Tampa, take Interstate 275 to Exit 25 (Downtown/West). Keep to the right at the fork in the ramp, then merge onto North Ashley Drive. The Tampa Museum of Art is less than a mile down North Ashley Drive, on the right.

"each **visit** will be **different** from the **one** before."

Hillsborough County – West Central Florida

Tampa Theatre

have you ever visited a palace?

Tampa Theatre

The architectural detail and grandeur of the Tampa Theatre is unparalleled in grand movie palaces.

the trip

We all love to go to the movies, but that simple excursion takes on a whole new meaning when you visit the magnificent Tampa Theatre. It is one of the nation's best-preserved examples of grand movie palace architecture. Built in 1926, it is listed on the National Register of Historic Places. In its early years, it presented extravagant vaudeville shows, concerts by its own orchestra and silent films.

what to see

Built as a silent film house by renowned architect John Eberson, the theater is a combination of Italian Renaissance, Byzantine, Greek Revival, English Tudor and more. It all works beautifully! The theater hosts some 700 events per year, including first-run and classic films, live shows, special events and tours.

other highlights

Part of your Tampa Theatre experience is seeing and hearing The Mighty Wurlitzer Organ. It has more than 1,000 pipes; some are 16-feet tall, others are the size of pencils. The theater also boasts incredibly ornate plasterwork and a design style described as "Florida-Mediterranean."

711 N. Franklin Street
Tampa, FL 33602
(813) 274-8981

Admission: *Film ticket prices: $6.25 adult non-members, $5.25 members, $4 seniors, military and students.*

Hours: *Check Web site, or call for film and event times.*

www.tampatheatre.org

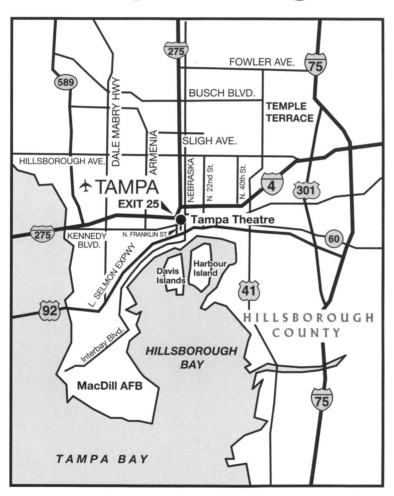

directions
From Tampa, take Interstate 275 to Exit 25 (Downtown/ West). Merge onto North Ashley Drive, then turn left onto East Zack Street. Park near the corner of Zack and Franklin streets (no cars are permitted on Franklin Street).

BayWalk

take a walk on the wonderful side

Pinellas County – West Central Florida

Restaurants, movies, shopping and entertainment – BayWalk is helping to change the face of downtown St. Pete.

Centro Ybor Associates

Centro Ybor Associates

the trip

BayWalk is the newest addition to blossoming downtown St. Petersburg, and it will turn your head! Muvico 20, a magnificent 20-screen theater, is the main focus for many visitors. But there's lots more, including dining, shopping, entertainment in the courtyard and live music on the weekends. The $40-million, 125,000-square-foot outdoor complex takes up an entire city block! And, as the name suggests, it's just a short walk to the Bay, where you can visit the renowned Museum of Fine Arts (255 Beach Drive N.E.) and the beautiful Sculpture Gardens.

what to see

For starters, kick back at Wet Willie's Daiquiri Bar (non-alcoholic beverages are available here too). You will get a birds-eye view of the crowd below from Willie's perch on the second floor. Want munchies? Rock out to a '50s burger and fries at Johnny Rockets. Or stop for a bite at TooJay's Gourmet Deli, a New York-style deli with a great selection of to-die-for pastries. At Dish, you get to choose your own ingredients, then have it cooked on one of the world's largest grills. If sports and good cuisine are your thing, huddle up at Dan Marino's Town Tavern. Next door is the always-packed Martini Bar.

other highlights

Visit fine retailers such as Ann Taylor, Five Fish, People's Pottery and Hurricane Pass, which carries tropical lines of clothing. It's Key Lime Confections for real Key lime products, fantastic ice cream and candies. If your feet start to hurt (even a little) stop at Mephisto's shoes. While in the neighborhood, take a stroll over to The Pier for more shops and eateries, like the world-famous Columbia Restaurant. Browse the shops at nearby Beach Drive.

BayWalk
Corner of First Street N. & Second Avenue N.
St. Petersburg, FL 33701
(727) 895-9277

Admission: *Free*

Hours: *Restaurant and shop hours vary. Call ahead for hours. For movie times and prices, call Muvico at (727) 502-0965 or check out the Web site at*
www.muvico.com

directions

From Tampa, take Interstate 275 south to Exit 10 (I-375). Merge onto Fourth Avenue North, then turn right onto Second Street North. BayWalk is to your left on the corner of First Street North and Second Avenue North. The parking garage is located on Second Street North; there is minimal parking on the street.

"serendipity in st. Pete!"

The Chattaway Restaurant

early St. Pete ambiance

H. Little

Dine alfresco amid the Cracker-style tubs planted with a colorful variety of Florida flowers.

The Chattaway Restaurant is famous for its mouth-watering "Chattaburgers" all-the-way.

Dakota Graphics

the trip

This taste-tempting landmark has been around for most of the 20th century and is happily headed into the 21st. The little wooden building once housed a grocery store, gas station and trolley stop. When the building changed hands in 1950, it was turned into a full-fledged restaurant and the Chattaway was born.

what to see

The Chattaway's casual charm is further embellished by an enclosed verandah and a rustic, old-time dining room. As for the food, try the famed "Chattaburger" (with all the fixings) and equally-famed onion rings. Many locals say it's the best burger in town.

other highlights

Be sure to ask about the daily specials. While waiting for your chow, take time to admire the huge collection of British collectibles throughout the restaurant.

358 22nd Avenue S.
St. Petersburg, FL 33705
(727) 823-1594

Admission: *Free. Prices of menu items may vary.*

Hours: *Open Monday through Friday 11 a.m. to 9:30 p.m., Saturday 8 a.m. to 9:30 p.m., Sunday 8 a.m. to 7:30 p.m.*

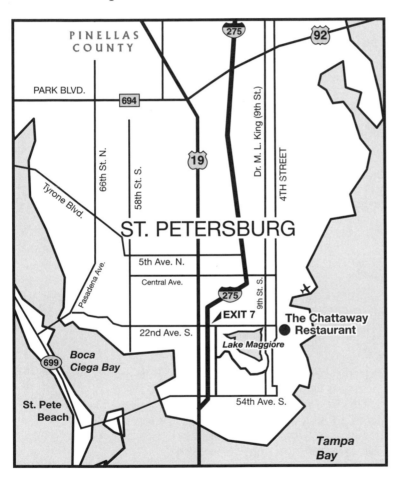

directions

From Tampa, take Interstate 275 South (toward Bradenton) to the 22nd Avenue South Exit (Exit 7). Head east all the way to 4th Street South. The Chattaway Restaurant is located on the southeast corner of 22nd Avenue South and Fourth Street South, across the street from Bartlett Park.

The Chattaway Restaurant

Florida Holocaust Museum

a time to remember

"Little Green Trees," from Samuel Bak's "Working Through the Past" Exhibit.

Florida Holocaust Museum

This piece is part of the "History, Heritage & Hope" Exhibit.

Florida Holocaust Museum

the trip

It is a journey of major historical significance at the Florida Holocaust Museum. As the fourth-largest Holocaust museum in the United States, it offers a powerful and sobering exploration of our past.

what to see

Here you will experience the dreams, achievements and convictions of the 11-million innocent victims of Nazi tyranny. The centerpiece here has a number — 1130695-5. It is one of the few remaining railroad boxcars used by the Nazi's to transport Jews to concentration camps. In another part of the museum are shoes that belonged to a two-year-old child who died with her mother in Auschwitz in 1943.

other highlights

Be sure to visit the wall of tiles, created mostly by children who have visited the museum. Part of the museum's education outreach includes The Speakers' Bureau, where Holocaust survivors, serving as eyewitnesses to history, share their stories. The museum also offers literature-based "Teaching Trunks," with lessons on the Holocaust for grades K through 12. The museum's Web site is the largest virtual holocaust museum in the world.

55 Fifth Street S.
St. Petersburg, FL 33701
(727) 820-0100

Admission: *$6 adults, $5 seniors and college students, $2 under 18. Discounts for groups of 10 or more by prior reservation.*

Hours: *Open Monday through Friday 10 a.m. to 5 p.m., Saturday and Sunday noon to 5 p.m. Closed Rosh Hashana, Yom Kippur and Christmas Day.*

www.flholocaustmuseum.org

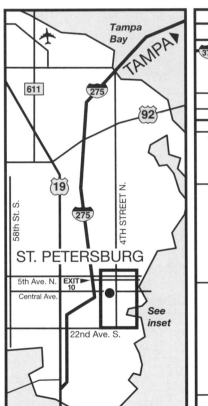

directions

From Tampa, take Interstate 275 south to Exit 10 (I-375) and follow the signs to Fourth Street North. Turn right onto Fifth Street North for about three and one-half blocks. Turn into the marked alley way directing you to the to parking lot. The museum is located at 55 Fifth Street South.

"images... that MUST never be forgotten."

Pinellas County – West Central Florida

Florida Orange Groves & Winery

wines with a twist

For the past 10 years the Shook family (l. to r.) Ray, Gladys and Vince, have been producing delicious citrus wines.

the trip

There's not a grape in the bunch at Florida's only citrus winery! The tours and tastings are always a treat and the gift shop is just packed with goodies.

what to see

Wines galore! But wait a minute. What's this? Cranberry, watermelon, tangerine and Key lime wine? That's right, and there's more, including the award-winning cherry, carrot and blackberry wines. Part of your tour includes a look at the Shook family's state-of-the-art winemaking operation. The Florida Citrus Commission recently awarded citrus winemakers the right to display the "Florida Sunshine Tree" logo on their labels. It's the first time that the Citrus Commission has allowed its mark on a beverage other than orange or grapefruit juice. A very nice boost for the Shook family.

other highlights

This winery is not only for oenophiles (i.e. wine lovers). There are plenty of other libations here, many without a hint of alcohol. Fresh orange and grapefruit juice are processed daily. While in the area, visit Ted Peters Smoked Fish restaurant just down the street, at 1350 Pasadena Ave., for some of the best smoked fish and burgers on the West Coast of Florida.

1500 Pasadena Avenue S.
St. Petersburg, FL 33707
Toll free: (800) 338-7923
(727) 347-4025

Admission: *Free. Prices of wines vary.*

Hours: *Open Monday through Saturday 9 a.m. to 5:30 p.m., Sunday noon to 5 p.m. in season (check for dates). Tastings available daily. Call for details and tour times.*

www.floridawine.com

directions

From Tampa, take Interstate 275 south to the Fifth Avenue North Exit (Exit 11) in St. Petersburg. Turn right (heading west) onto Fifth Avenue North and go to 66th Street North. Turn left (south) on 66th Street North which will then turn into Pasadena Avenue. Continue south, past Ted Peters Smoked Fish restaurant on the left. You will see the winery on the same side of the street, just before the causeway to St. Pete Beach.

"Pinellas County's only winery!"

Florida Orange Groves & Winery

Pinellas County – West Central Florida

browsing by the beach

Folks travel far and wide to view the collection of art at the Vincent William Gallery.

Check out the unique merchandise at the Five & Dime store, a Corey Avenue mainstay.

the trip

Just a stone's throw from the sands of St. Pete Beach, we come across a shopping experience that is both unique and personal. Historic Corey Avenue has it all, including restaurants, clothing, gift and beach shops, a church thrift shop and foreign first-run movies.

what to see

Find out what the word is on the street at Scottie's News & Card Shop. Locals have been dropping in here for their daily dose of national and international news for more than 40 years. Then head to the ever-thrifty Corey Avenue Five & Dime store, where aisle after aisle is loaded with plain-old great stuff. For a bit more than a nickel or a dime, treat yourself to Lithos Jewelry, where you will find the work of international designers. And, in a nifty gift shop called Simply Perfect, you can browse through the collectible Boyds Bears. In the mood for a fresh-brewed cup of cappuccino? The Coffee Cottage has a little bit of everything. And everything is for sale, including the tables and chairs ... no kidding!

other highlights

Built in 1939 by Boston financier Stephen Girard for "a mere $50,000," the landmark art deco St. Pete Beach Theatre shows "cutting edge" independent and foreign first-run films.

Corey Avenue
Downtown St. Pete Beach
74th Avenue off Gulf Boulevard
St. Pete Beach, FL 33706
(727) 360-8683

Admission: *Free*

Hours: *Restaurant and shop hours vary.*

www.coreyave.com

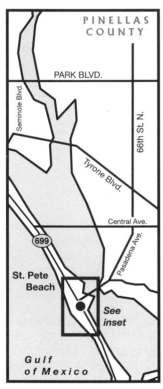

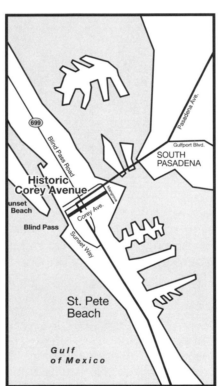

directions
From Tampa, take Interstate 275 to Exit 11 (Fifth Avenue North), then turn right (west) onto Fifth Avenue North and follow to 66th Street North, which becomes Pasadena Avenue. Follow Pasadena past Ted Peters Smoked Fish restaurant on the left, then go over the bridge until it turns into 75th Avenue. Turn left onto Mangrove Avenue, then right onto Corey Avenue. Parking is available on the street and in area parking lots.

"a splendid adventure!"

John's Pass Village

it takes a village!

Pinellas County – West Central Florida

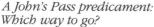
A John's Pass predicament: Which way to go?

St. Pete/CW Convention Bureau

St. Pete/CW Convention Bureau

Old Glory waves proudly over the John's Pass Boardwalk.

the trip

At first glance you might think you've arrived at an old New England fishing village. It certainly has all the rustic charm. But quaint John's Pass Village is a lot more than that. It's a bonanza of retail, recreational and restaurant venues.

what to see

Along the boardwalk there are many days' worth of things to see and do. Jack's Marina is one of several places offering boat and watercraft rentals. You can go parasailing, deep-sea fishing, shell hunting, sailing and even dolphin watching. And, if you feel lucky, the casino boats are here too, offering daily excursions. Hungry? The seafood restaurants are outstanding. Sculley's is one of many dining establishments ready to soothe that savage appetite. The Friendly Fisherman has also been luring locals for years. For real New York-style pizza, stop at DeLosa's Pizzeria right at the entrance to the boardwalk.

other highlights

Gift shops abound, including FLA Mingos, Raptors and Relics, Sugar Daddy's, Wild Time and the Unique Boutique. One of the new arrivals on the boardwalk is Thomas Kinkade Gallery, featuring the works of the beloved "Painter of Light."

John's Pass Village & Boardwalk
12901 Gulf Boulevard E.
Madeira Beach, FL 33708

Gulf Beaches
Chamber of Commerce
(800) 944-1847

Admission: *Free*

Hours: *Shop and restaurant hours vary.*

directions

From Tampa, take Interstate 275 south to Exit 15 (Gandy Boulevard/C.R. 694), then turn left (south) at Seminole Boulevard (S.R. 595). As the road splits, stay to the left towards Madeira Beach. Turn left (south) onto Gulf Boulevard, then left into John's Pass Village before the bridge. (John's Pass is directly across from the Gulf of Mexico).

"you won't get bored on the boardwalk."

Pinellas County – West Central Florida

Marine Life Adventures

an interactive marine experience

Adventurers learn about marine biology in the mud flats.

Lisa Shimatzki

Marianne Klingel

A young adventurer examines the catch of the otter trawl before releasing it to the Bay.

the trip

Here's your opportunity to explore Florida's waters with genuine marine biologists. It's a great way to learn something new while having fun! Adventures can last a few hours, or days. It's your call. The Marine Life Adventures Program is sponsored by the nationally-acclaimed Clearwater Marine Aquarium.

what to see

It's wonderful! You'll surround yourself with the sea, its creatures, and the beautiful, natural environment. You will learn why this area is vital to plankton, sea snails, spider crabs, crown conch and other marine life. What a marvelous way to spend some great time on the water, while learning about it, above and below.

other highlights

Camping trips on the Spoil Islands offer a unique way to study tides and nocturnal animals. The islands were created years ago by Army engineers as they dredged the channel in the Intracoastal Waterway. The excursions are geared for people of all ages and interests.

Clearwater Marine Aquarium
249 Windward Passage
Clearwater, FL 33767
Toll free: (888) 239-9414
(727) 441-1790

Admission: *Call for times and rates.*

Hours: *The aquarium is open Monday through Friday 9 a.m. to 5 p.m., Saturday 9 a.m. to 4 p.m., Sunday 11 a.m. to 4 p.m.*

www.cmaquarium.com

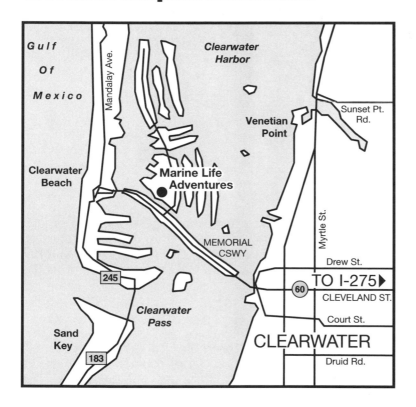

directions

From Tampa, take Interstate 275 south to S.R. 60 (west). Cross over the Courtney Campbell Causeway which becomes Gulf-to-Bay Boulevard and then Cleveland Street. Once over the causeway, turn right (north) onto Island Way. Turn left at Windward Passage to park and enjoy the Clearwater Marine Aquarium.

" the most beautiful classroom you will ever see."

Memphis Gold

where Elvis still reigns

Memphis Gold

Memphis Gold

Memphis Gold boasts the largest Elvis Presley collection south of Memphis.

Pinellas County – West Central Florida

the trip

In the lovely town of Dunedin, we found the largest selection of Elvis Presley memorabilia this side of Memphis. Even if you're not a collector, this is an absolutely remarkable place to visit. Owner Jerry Theriault has been collecting Elvis items since 1957. You will be astonished at all the items you can see and purchase.

what to see

You will find about 3,000 different collectibles, with many more added weekly. Jerry, who you may notice resembles "a certain someone," boasts about 700 items not found at Graceland! You will see things like a bottle of Elvis wine imported from Italy, an original newspaper headline from the day Elvis died in 1977, Elvis wall clocks in various colors, a 24-karat gold-plated record and plenty of clothing that you simply *must* add to your wardrobe.

other highlights

Jerry can give you the scoop on what it was like to see Elvis in concert. He saw Elvis perform more than 85 times! He's also a guy who's never too busy to talk about the "King." Hound dogs hungry for more rare and expensive collectibles should check out Jerry's online catalog.

1143 Main Street
Dunedin, FL 34698
(727) 738-8412

Admission: *Free. Prices of items vary.*

Hours: *Open Tuesday through Saturday 11 a.m. to 6 p.m., Sunday noon to 5 p.m. Closed Monday.*

www.memphisgold.com

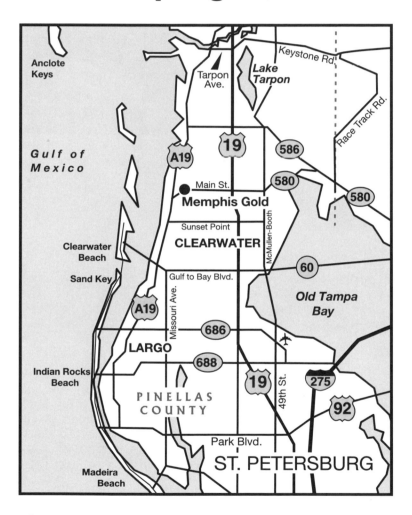

directions

From Tampa, take S.R. 60 west to U.S. 19. Turn right and head north to S.R. 580. Turn left on S.R. 580 (Main Street) and go west for about two miles to Memphis Gold.

The Town of Safety Harbor

the secret by the Bay

© Sue Suby, Tropical Breeze Publications, Inc.

© Sue Suby, Tropical Breeze Publications, Inc.

The elegant facade of the Safety Harbor Resort & Spa sets the tone for the pampering to follow.

Pinellas County – West Central Florida

the trip

It may be the Town of Safety Harbor, but a glance at the "new" look of Main Street and you get the feeling of a quaint little village. The world-famous Safety Harbor Resort & Spa, a magnet for many celebrities, stands at the east end of Main.

what to see

There are more than 40 shops and restaurants and several lovely parks. Spend some time enjoying the beauty of the waterfront at the city marina. Across the street is the Safety Harbor Museum, where they say you can experience "10,000 years of history." Farther down Main Street, stop at Syd Entel Galleries, a Safety Harbor mainstay for 20 years. The visual celebration continues next door at Susan Benjamin Glass. Original painting, sculptures and signed prints are a veritable feast for the eyes.

other highlights

There are a variety of cuisines represented here. It's just a matter of selecting the right one to satisfy your cravings. Try Cello's Charhouse restaurant, then head over to Chantilly Cakes for dessert. There's lots more. Just be sure to leave your calorie counter in the car!

Safety Harbor
Chamber of Commerce
200 Main Street
Safety Harbor, FL 34695
(727) 726-2890

Admission: *Free*

Hours: *Shop and restaurant hours vary.*

www.safetyharborchamber.com

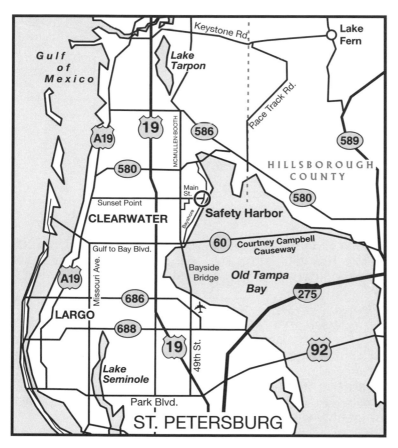

directions

From Tampa, take S.R. 60 west to Clearwater over the Courtney Campbell Causeway which becomes Gulf to Bay Boulevard. Bear to the right (north) on McMullen-Booth Road to Main Street. Turn right (east) onto Main Street and follow to the center of the town of Safety Harbor.

"all **signs** point **to** a **fun** day in Safety Harbor."

The Town of Safety Harbor

Shell Key

like Gilligan's Island, but you get to go home

Hop aboard for a trip to the sparkling white sands of Shell Key.

the trip

From St. Pete Beach's Merry Pier, take a 10-minute catamaran shuttle to Shell Key. It's a beautiful, unspoiled barrier island just south of Pass-a-Grille, at the southern end of St. Pete Beach.

what to see

You might have guessed that Shell Key got its name because it's a great place to find some spectacular shells. But there's plenty else to do, like watching the birds (the Key is a bird preservation area). Sunbathing and snorkeling are also high on the list. You can rent beach umbrellas, snorkels and masks, but bring your own cooler and a bag for collecting shells. And check out the shell chart on your way back from the Key to identify your finds!

other highlights

Back on dry land, pop across the street and enjoy Historic Pass-a-Grille's Eighth Avenue. You can browse several shops and drop in for lunch or dinner at the Eighth Avenue Fish House & Grille. For breakfast, head slightly west to the Gulf to enjoy a fresh fruit plate or full English breakfast at the outdoor Seaside Grill (900 Gulf Way), located directly on the Gulf of Mexico.

Merry Pier at Pass-a-Grille
801 Pass-a-Grille Way
St. Pete Beach, FL 33706
(727) 360-1348

Admission: *Round-trip shuttle fares: $12 adults, $6 children 12 and under.*

Hours: *The Shell Key Shuttle departs from Merry Pier daily at 10 a.m., noon, and 2 p.m. and returns at 12:15 p.m., 2:15 p.m., and 4:15 p.m.*

www.shellkeyshuttle.com

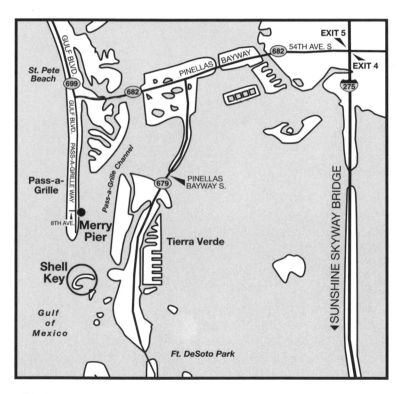

directions

From Tampa, take Interstate 275 south to Exit 5 (Pinellas Bayway/St. Pete Beach/S.R. 682). Go about three miles (through the toll booth) to Gulf Boulevard. Turn left and follow Gulf Boulevard, which becomes Pass-a-Grille Way. Follow to the Merry Pier which is on Pass-a-Grille Channel at 8th Avenue on the left side of the road. Park on the street, but be sure to check your meter!

"a Shell hunter's dream."

Pinellas County – West Central Florida

Suncoast Seabird Sanctuary

this hospital is for the birds

Stan Ashbrook

These baby Eastern brown pelicans were hatched in the safety of the sanctuary.

Ernie Simmons

the trip

The Suncoast Seabird Sanctuary is the largest wild bird hospital in the nation. Founded in 1971 by zoologist Ralph Heath, Jr., the sanctuary rescues, treats and releases sick and injured wild birds. Unfortunately, business has been booming.

what to see

You can see more than 600 birds, including egrets, cormorants, brown pelicans and various birds of prey. On an average day, Ralph and the folks at the sanctuary treat about two dozen birds injured by gunshots, fishing hooks and lines. While the sanctuary's goal is to release the birds after they have recuperated from their injuries, some who have lost an eye or a limb remain here in permanent residence.

other highlights

Every bird at the Sanctuary is special. But "Pelican Pat," here for 30 years, is unique. On the day she was brought in, actor Pat O'Brien was visiting the sanctuary and took a particular interest in her. And that's how she got her name. Pat was a mess — a fishhook in one eye and a wing badly cut by fishing line. She looked pretty rough. But she survived and is still here for all to see, and love.

18328 Gulf Boulevard
Indian Shores, FL 33785
(727) 391-6211

Admission: *Free. Contributions are appreciated.*

Hours: *Open daily 9 a.m. to sunset.*

www.seabirdsanctuary.org

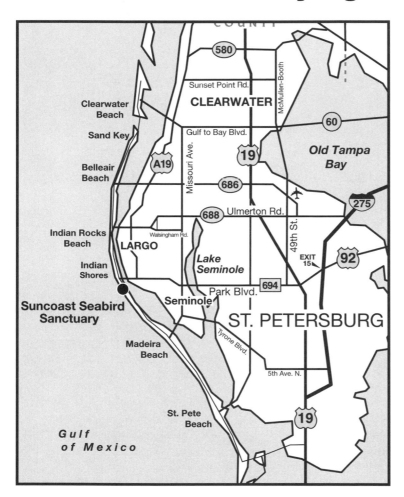

directions

From Tampa, take Interstate 275 south to Exit 15 (C.R. 694). Merge onto Gandy Boulevard North, which becomes Park Boulevard. Go about 10 miles and turn left onto Gulf Boulevard. The Suncoast Seabird Sanctuary is less than a mile down on the right in Indian Shores.

"**this** is a **wonderful** daytime destination, and **you'll** never know **what** surprises **await.**"

Pinellas County – West Central Florida

Sunken Gardens
a tropical downtown paradise

Resident parrots Joey and Moosey appear to enjoy the spectacular beauty of Sunken Gardens as much as everyone else.

Sunken Gardens

Sunken Gardens

the trip
Not so long ago, this landmark attraction drew 300,000 visitors a year. But because of declining attendance, the owners opted to sell the place. That could have meant the end of Sunken Gardens. But St. Petersburg voters gave thumbs up for the city to buy and operate the Gardens. And now, the transformation from an "attraction" to an educational and cultural center is complete.

what to see
Check out the Gardens' latest additions. There are more than 6,000 new plants, a new butterfly garden and aviary. There's also a new rain forest information center where you'll see some remarkable critters, like snakes and green lizards. Yet, much of the old Sunken Gardens remains. It just wouldn't be the same without Free Spirit, the majestic bald eagle who has made this place home for 15 years...or those kooky parrots, Joey and Moosey! Some things never change.

other highlights
Guided tours are given Wednesday through Sunday at 10:30 a.m. and 1:30 p.m. This is one of the best bargains around!

1825 Fourth Street N.
St. Petersburg, FL 33701
(727) 551-3100

Admission: *$4 adults, $3 senior, $1 children ages 3-12.*

Hours: *Wednesday through Sunday 10 a.m. to 4 p.m. Guided tours are given Wednesday through Sunday at 10:30 a.m. and 1:30 p.m.*

www.sunkengardens.com

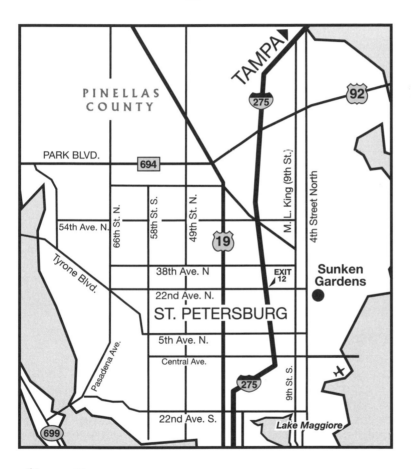

directions

From Tampa, take Interstate 275 South to St. Petersburg. Take Exit 12 (22nd Avenue North). Turn left and head east on 22nd Avenue North and follow it to Fourth Street North. Turn right on Fourth Street North. Sunken Gardens is less than a half-mile on the left.

"you'll be **awed** by the beauty and **tranquility** of these **lovely** gardens."

Sunken Gardens

Florida Gulf Coast Railroad Museum

all aboard!

Manatee County – West Central Florida

Florida Gulf Coast Railroad Museum

Florida Gulf Coast Railroad Museum

Built in 1951 and donated to the museum by the Department of Defense, both the #1822 and #1835, which sports the Florida Gulf Coast Museum logo, are 1500 horsepower locomotives.

the trip

Train lovers—get ready! You will ride through rustic Manatee County prairie land on this moving exhibit. Operated entirely by volunteers, the museum was founded in 1981 to acquire, protect and operate historic examples of the line. It opened in 1903 as the Florida & West Indies Railroad & Steamship Company.

what to see

These diesel-powered trains include open-window coaches, air-conditioned coach and lounge cars, and cabooses. From Parrish, your trip takes you to Willow, once the location of a large logging mill. Farther along, the train stops at Nichols Station, surrounded by cypress trees in a swamp that seems out of place in this prairie setting. Keep an eye out for alligators, deer, turtles and many birds along the way. And depending on the day, you might even encounter masked bandits!

other highlights

Want more fun? The museum will rent you a locomotive on an hourly basis, complete with an instructor to show you how to operate the controls. After a brief instruction period, you'll be running the locomotive yourself! When finished, you receive an honorary locomotive engineer certificate suitable for framing.

U.S. 301 & 83rd Street E.
Parrish, FL 34219
Toll free: (877) 869-0800
(941) 776-0906

Admission: *$10 adults, $6 ages 2 through 11. Call for group rates. Locomotive rental: $50 to $75 per hour, depending on the type of train. Reservations required.*

Hours: *Trains depart 1 p.m. and 3 p.m. Sunday, May through September; 11 a.m. and 1 p.m. Saturday, and 1 p.m. and 3 p.m. Sunday, October through April.*

www.fgcrrm.org

directions

From Tampa, take Interstate 75 south to Exit 45 (Moccasin Wallow Road/S.R. 683). Head east toward U.S. 301 for about five miles. Turn right (south) on U.S. 301 and go about one-quarter of a mile. Turn left at 83rd Street East. Go one short block to the parking lot.

"**for** the **Casey Jones** **in** all **of** us."

Manatee County – West Central Florida

J.P. Igloo Ice & Inline Sports Complex

cool refuge in the sub-tropical climate

J. P. Igloo

Skate yourself into a cool mood at J.P. Igloo. Ice hockey, anyone?

J. P. Igloo

the trip

This 115,000-square-foot family and entertainment complex includes not one, but two NHL-size ice skating rinks and a U.S.A. Hockey in-line rink. This is year-round fun, and wonderfully cool in those hot Florida summer months.

what to see

Skating is the main attraction here. But that does not mean the fun begins and ends on the rinks. A fitness center, where you can pay by the day or become a member, overlooks both ice rinks. Very cool! There's an indoor extreme-skate park, full-service pro shop, conference and corporate meeting facilities, and a restaurant. J.P. Igloo also offers figure skating, ice hockey, soccer, in-line skating, ballet, and other dance programs and classes.

other highlights

Hey kids, check out the video arcade! And parents, after you drop off the youngsters, shop till you drop at the huge Prime Outlets Mall next door.

5309 29th Street E.
Ellenton, FL 34222
(941) 723-3663

Admission: *$6 ice skating and inline skating, $3 skate rental. Discounts for groups of 30 or more. Call for fitness center, dance program and class fees.*

Hours: *Call for rink, dance programs, and class times.*

www.jpigloo.com

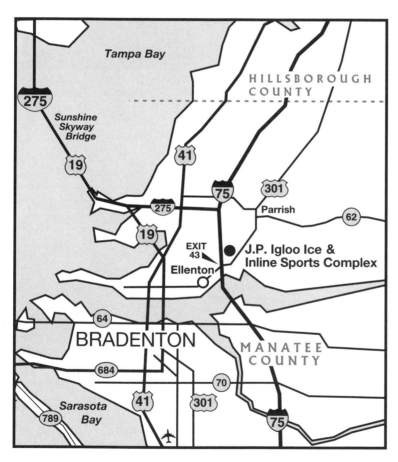

directions

From Tampa, head south on Interstate 75 to Exit 43 (U.S. 301/Ellenton/Palmetto). Merge left onto U.S. 301 North. Turn left onto 60th Avenue East, then turn left again onto 29th Street East to J.P. Igloo. (J.P. Igloo is located next to the Prime Outlet Mall).

" there **is** a **lot** going on under the **dome.**"

J.P. Igloo Ice & Inline Sports Complex

Manatee County – West Central Florida

Roaring 20's Pizza & Pipes

a tasty, easy-on-the-ears destination

Roaring 20s Pizza and Pipes

The Mighty Wurlitzer is a sight and sound to behold.

Roaring 20s Pizza and Pipes

the trip
At Ellenton's Roaring 20's the main focus is twofold— mighty good pizza and The Mighty Wurlitzer organ. This is a remarkable one-of-a-kind place.

what to see
"Food first," is my slogan. And as you will see, the names of the pizzas set the tone for this place—The Charlie Chaplin, The Buster Keaton, The Bees Knees and The Mighty Wurlitzer—wait until you see what they put on this pie! Not in the mood for pizza? Try a sandwich or a pasta selection, and finish your feast with a big scoop of ice cream.

other highlights
Now on to the other star of the show — the music! The Mighty Wurlitzer began its life at Oakland's Paramount Theatre in 1931, and found its way here in 1999. It was no easy task. It took 2,600 hours to rebuild, then another 1,700 to install the 16-ton organ. A 20 horsepower blower supplies air for its 3,000 pipes. Amazingly, the Wurlitzer has 26 miles of wiring and 350 controls! Also, good luck trying to stump the organists with what you think is an unusual song request. These guys know just about everything! Talk about a great family destination!

6750 N. U.S. 301
Ellenton, FL 34222
(941) 723-1733

Admission: *Free. Prices of menu items vary.*

Hours: *Open Monday through Thursday 4:30 p.m. to 9 p.m., Friday 4:30 p.m. to 10 p.m., Saturday noon to 2:30 p.m. and 4:30 p.m. to 10 p.m., Sunday noon to 2:30 p.m. and 4:30 p.m. to 9 p.m.*

www.roaring20spizza.com

"your Roaring 20's experience should be a roaring success."

directions

From Tampa, head south on Interstate 75 to Exit 43 (U.S. 301/Ellenton/Palmetto). Merge left onto U.S. 301 North, then follow the road for about three-quarters of a mile. Roaring 20's Pizza and Pipes is on the north side of U.S. 301.

Rosa Fiorelli Winery

full-bodied adventure

Rosa Fiorelli Winery

A newly expanded building accommodates wine tasting, weddings and other festive functions.

The Fiorellis proudly display their award-winning wines.

Rosa Fiorelli Winery

Manatee County – West Central Florida

the trip

It started out as five rows of grapes in the backyard. Today, it has swelled to ten grand acres! It all began when Rosa and Antonio Fiorelli relocated here from Sicily and opened Manatee County's first winery on a quiet little road in Bradenton, just south of Lake Manatee.

what to see

Your visit will include a tour of the vineyard. You will learn about the different varieties of grapes, growth seasons, pruning and harvesting times. Then see how grapes are crushed, pressed, fermented and bottled. All followed up with a little wine-tasting.

other highlights

Bring home some *vino!* Depending on the season, eight different varieties are available, from the full-bodied Manatee Red to the sweet Florida Muscadine, nicknamed the "*amoré* wine," or "love wine." Their *Blanc du Bois Classico* was a Silver Medal winner at the 1999 Indianapolis International Commercial Wine Competition.

4020 County Road 675
Bradenton, FL 34202
(941) 322-0976

Admission: *Lunch Tours, which include a souvenir wine glass, are $11.50 per person, including gratuity. Snack Tours are $5.50 per person. Regular Tours of the winery and vineyards are $2 per person. Prices of wines vary.*

Hours: *Monday through Saturday 10 a.m. to 6 p.m., Sunday noon to 5 p.m.*

www.floridawinery.com

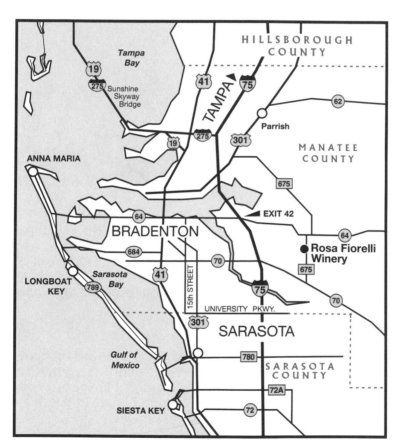

directions

From Tampa, take Interstate 75 south to Exit 42 (S.R. 64). Go east about 10 miles to C.R. 675. Turn right (south), then head south on C.R. 675 to the winery.

"a tasty mom-and-pop operation."

Rosa Fiorelli Winery

Royal Lipizzan
Stallions of Austria

extraordinary grace

Manatee County – West Central Florida

Bill Murphy

Bill Murphy

For three months out of each year, hundreds of equine lovers flock to see the Lipizzan Stallions learn their routine.

the trip

You can see these magnificent horses in training for only the first three months of the year. And while it may look like a real performance, part of the training of the young stallions is to get comfortable in front of an audience. It all takes place under the close direction of Colonel Ottomar Herrmann, whose family has trained the Lipizzans for more than 300 years.

what to see

This is a rare opportunity to see the magnificent Royal Lipizzans up close. The stallions were saved from almost certain extinction at the end of World War II. Colonel Herrmann and his father smuggled their horses out of Europe under the protection of General George S. Patton. Decades later, these "original" Lipizzans are here for all to behold!

other highlights

It takes nine years for these horses to learn "the capriole," the move for which they are best known. Leaping from all four feet, they strike out with the hind legs. Once a battle maneuver of their ancestors, it is now part of this remarkable equine ballet.

32755 Singletary Road
Myakka City, FL 34251
(941) 322-1501
(941) 322-2539

Admission: *Free. Reservations suggested for groups of 15 or more. Remember, you can only see these magnificent horses in training during the first three months of the year.*

Hours: *Seasonal. Winter training sessions begin the first week after Christmas through the end of March. Thursday and Friday at 3 p.m., Saturday at 10 a.m.* **Call ahead to confirm.**

www.herrmannslipizzans.com

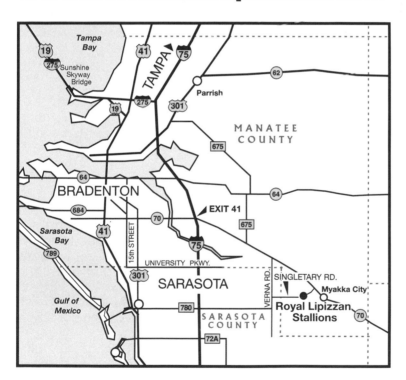

directions
From Tampa, take Interstate 75 south to Exit 41 (S.R. 70 Bradenton/Arcadia), merging onto S.R. 70. Head southeast on S.R. 70 for about 12 miles, then turn right on Verna Road. Take a left (go east) on Singletary Road and follow to the Royal Lipizzan Stallion Ranch.

"the **training** takes years, **beginning** when they **turn** three."

Sarasota County – West Central Florida

The Ringling Museum

two museums in one

"Hager and the Angel" (1637) in the Ringling Art Museum.

The Ringling Museum

the trip

Talk about a feast for the eyes! There are more than five centuries of European art in the Art Museum, including a world-famous collection of 17th century baroque paintings. The nearby Museum of the Circus honors John Ringling and celebrates the success of the Ringling Bros. and Barnum & Bailey Circus.

what to see

A testament to John and Mable Ringling's love of art, the Art Museum is considered one of the most beautiful in the nation. John Ringling, an influential business tycoon and cultural baron of his day, bequeathed his valuable and extensive art collection, palazzo, gardens and grounds to the people of Florida. The 19th century art is splendid, and the museum actively collects 20th century and contemporary art. In the courtyard — a wonder to behold — bronze replicas of Baroque, Greek and Roman sculptures represent the nation's most complete collection of works by the Chiurazzi foundry in Naples, Italy.

other highlights

You will find the story of "The Greatest Show on Earth" in the Circus Museum. This is the first museum of its kind, with a collection that documents the history of the circus. Here you will see an antique parade wagon used to delight children in the 1920s and 1930s. Also on display are posters, costumes, handbills and miniature circuses. While there, be sure to visit the Ca' d'Zan, John Ringling's magnificent winter residence featured in our first **One Tank Trips** book.

5401 Bay Shore Road
Sarasota, FL 34243
(941) 359-5700
(941) 351-1660

Admission: *$9 adults, $8 ages 55 and over.*

Hours: *Open daily 10 a.m. to 5:30 p.m.
Closed Thanksgiving, Christmas and New Year's Day.*

www.ringling.org

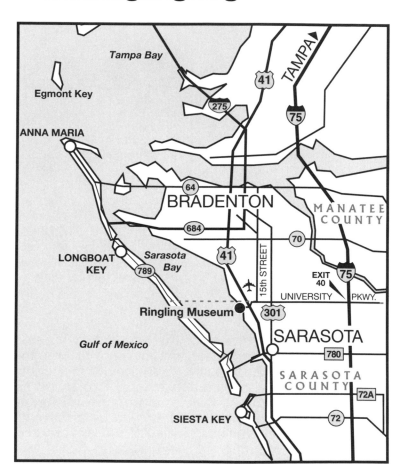

directions

From Tampa, take Interstate 75 south to Exit 40. Merge onto University Parkway and follow to the end. The Ringling Museum is at the end of University Parkway which becomes Ringling Plaza.

"a three-ring **experience.**"

The Ringling Museum

The Florida Keys & Key West

Crane Point Hammock

the essence of the Florida Keys

Beautiful dioramas depict the history of the Keys.

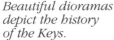

Sam Kennedy

Sam Kennedy

Iguana "Wild Willie" is a favorite attraction at the Museum of Natural History of the Florida Keys.

the trip

This is a fascinating and unique 63-acre site. It's home to the Museum of Natural History, Children's Museum, Adderley Town Historic Site and Marathon's Wild Bird Center. It includes an extensive nature trail system leading through a dense tropical forest to a spectacular view of Florida Bay.

what to see

Inside the museum, explore the history of the Keys. You will see a 600-year-old canoe crafted from a single log used by Key Indians in the 17th century and a Bellarmine jug from the 1500s, found in 1980 in near-perfect condition. You will also learn about Henry Flagler and his eight-year saga of building the Overseas Railroad from Miami to Key West. Completed in 1912, the railroad was destroyed by a powerful hurricane in 1935. You will see remnants of the railroad as you drive over the Seven Mile Bridge in Marathon, the longest in the Keys.

other highlights

A stop at the Children's Museum is a must for the kids. Here, they can climb aboard an interactive 17th-century galleon, "Los Niños de Los Cayos." Youngsters can also examine sea creatures in "touch tanks." To absorb the natural beauty of the Keys, take a walk along the boardwalk, part of the nearly three miles of nature trails.

Mile Marker 50.5
5550 Overseas Highway (U.S. 1)
Marathon, FL 33052
(305) 743-9100
(305) 743-7142

Admission: *$7.50 adults, $6 ages 65 and over, $4 students, children under 6 are free.*

Hours: *Open Monday through Saturday 9 a.m. to 5 p.m., Sunday noon to 5 p.m.*

www.cranepoint.org

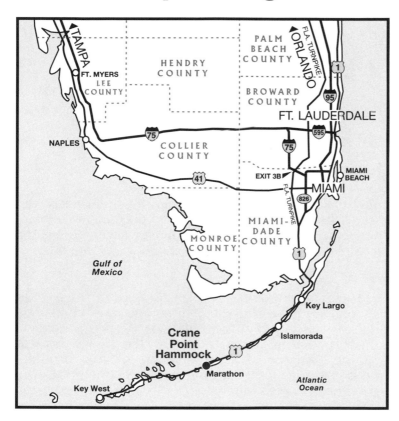

directions

From Tampa, take Interstate 75 south to Exit 3B (Turnpike South) and merge onto the Florida Turnpike. Turn right onto South Dixie Highway which becomes U.S. 1 (Overseas Highway). Follow U.S. 1 about 70 miles to Crane Point Hammock.

"a chance to see the Keys as they once were."

John Pennekamp Coral Reef State Park

the underwater spectacle in the Upper Keys

The Florida Keys & Key West

John Pennekamp State Park

John Pennekamp State Park

Explore the magic of the underwater world.

John Pennekamp State Park

the trip

John Pennekamp Coral Reef State Park is America's first underwater park. Scuba diving or snorkeling offers a unique opportunity to explore all the magic this amazing underwater world has to offer. You will see everything from incredible coral formations to vibrant, colorful fish.

what to see

Formed in the 1960s, Pennekamp Park encompasses more than 100-square miles of mangrove shoreline, grass flats and coral reef. Adjacent to Pennekamp is the Key Largo National Marine Sanctuary. Both of these pristine coral reef areas are protected by law against environmental abuse, assuring the preservation of this beautiful resource. If diving is not your thing, try snorkeling. They've got all the gear you need right there! There's plenty for landlubbers too. Log some beach time, walk along the beautiful mangrove trail, canoe, kayak or pitch a tent at one of 47 camping sites.

other highlights

Located underwater at Key Largo Dry Rocks Reef is the "Christ of the Deep," a nine-foot tall bronze statue symbolizing peace among mankind. It is one of the most well-known dive and snorkeling attractions in all the Florida Keys.

Mile Marker 102.5
Overseas Highway (U.S. 1)
Key Largo, FL 33036
(305) 451-1202
(305) 451-1621

Admission: *Tour, courses, boat and equipment rental prices vary.*

Hours: *Snorkeling tours depart daily at 9 a.m., noon and 3 p.m. Scuba courses begin at 9 a.m.*

www.pennekamppark.com

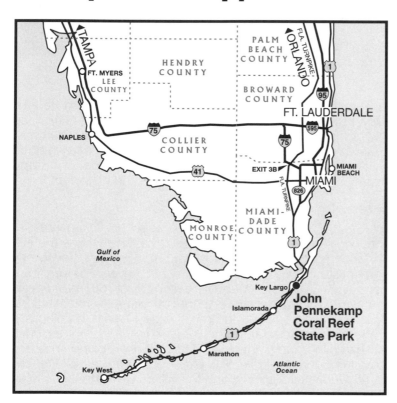

directions

From Tampa, take Interstate 75 to Exit 3B (Turnpike South) and merge onto the Florida Turnpike. Turn right onto South Dixie Highway which becomes U.S. 1 (Overseas Highway). Follow U.S. 1 to the green and white Mile Marker 102.5. A left turn at Mile Marker 102.5 takes you to John Pennekamp Coral Reef State Park.

"the fish, the water... a celebration of colors."

Key West at Daytime

a place for parrotheads

The Florida Keys & Key West

Enjoy a comprehensive tour of Key West on the famous Conch Tour Train.

Stuart Newman Associates

Stuart Newman Associates

the trip

Key West is about so many things. And that includes getting from here to there...in no hurry. Just about anything and everything seems to take place on this Key, which is the southernmost tip of the United States. The days, however, are somewhat more subdued compared to the wild party nights. Take in all the fun of Duval Street, or simply cruise the network of historic streets teeming with interesting architecture, rich foliage and brilliant blooms.

what to see

On Duval Street, get your "cheeseburger in paradise" at Margaritaville. Owner and Florida singing legend Jimmy Buffett occasionally joins the live band on stage for a song or two. Next door is Fast Buck Freddie's, Key West's incredible department store. If you feel like rockin', head over to Sloppy Joe's for a rollicking happy hour, or to the legendary Green Parrot (601 Whitehead St.) where folks have gathered for more than 100 years. If you want to kick back, relax and enjoy a sumptuous meal. Blue Heaven on Thomas Street (roosters and all) is a delectable choice. Its colorful history includes cockfighting and gambling. Now there are Friday night boxing matches refereed by an Ernest Hemingway look-alike. Other great choices: for French, Café des Artistes; for Cuban, El Siboney; and for Italian, La Trattoria.

other highlights

Enjoy a tour of the Hemingway House, where the famous author wrote many of his novels. Check out the six-toed cats; they are everywhere! For something off-the-beaten track, take the Key West Cemetery tour and discover who's behind (and under) the raised coffins and quirky tombstone inscriptions. Bring home some Key lime juice from the Conch Tour Train Gift Shop, where you can also purchase tickets for a comprehensive train tour of Key West.

Key West Chamber of Commerce
402 Wall Street
Key West, FL 33040
(305) 294-2587

Admission: *Free. Museum and tour rates vary.*

Hours: *Restaurant, shop and museum hours vary.*

www.keywestchamber.org

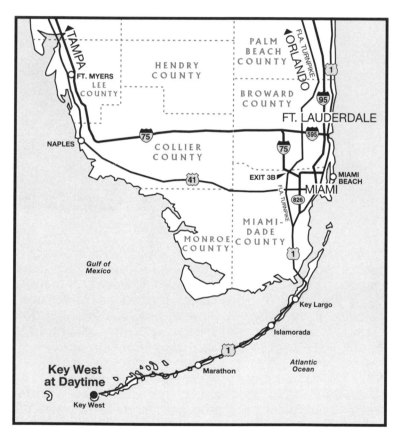

directions

From Tampa, take Interstate 75 to Exit 3B (Turnpike South) and merge onto the Florida Turnpike. Turn right onto South Dixie Highway which becomes U.S. 1 (Overseas Highway). Follow U.S. 1 for about 120 miles to Key West. Turn right onto North Roosevelt Boulevard which becomes Truman Avenue. Follow Truman Avenue, then turn right onto Duval Street, Key West's busiest street.

there's no **place** like it in the **world."**

Key West at Sunset Celebration

an evening fun fest

You'll get caught up in the carnival atmosphere in Key West.

Stuart Newman Associates

the trip

Many noted figures have enjoyed the sunset from Mallory Square over the years (Audubon wrote about it in the early 1800s). But the actual celebration began in the 1960s when carefree souls would go there to "watch Atlantis arising out of the cloud formations at sunset." Nowadays, musicians, artists, jugglers, clowns, psychics, food vendors and tourists gather every evening in Mallory Square to celebrate the close of another day in the tropical paradise known as Key West.

what to see

The celebration is an incubator for the arts and a launching pad for visual and performing art careers. Talented performers like Dominique the Catman, tightrope walker Will Soto, and "Parrot Bill's Bird Show" have been amazing folks at Key West sunsets for more than 20 years. Witness the Great Rondini's mind-boggling escape from chains and a strait jacket, while suspended upside down.

other highlights

Not to be overlooked are the countless arts and crafts exhibitors and food vendors. Feast your eyes on everything from jewelry to body art while gobbling down moist conch fritters, spicy Jamaican meat patties, fresh shrimp kabobs and other gastronomic delights.

Mallory Square
Key West, FL 33040

Cultural Preservation Society
P.O. Box 4837
Key West, FL 33041
(305) 292-7700

Admission: *Free*

Hours: *The Sunset Celebration begins two hours before sunset every night.*

www.sunsetcelebration.org

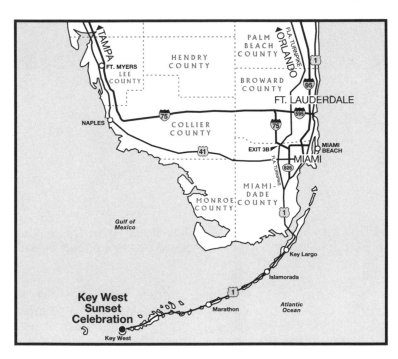

directions

From Tampa, take Interstate 75 to Exit 3B (Turnpike South) and merge onto the Florida Turnpike. Turn right onto South Dixie Highway which becomes U.S. 1 (Overseas Highway). Follow U.S. 1 for about 120 miles to Key West. Turn right onto North Roosevelt Boulevard which becomes Truman Avenue. Follow Truman Avenue and turn right on Duval Street. Take Duval to Front Street which overlooks Key West Harbor.

"you'll get caught up in the carnival atmosphere."

The Florida Keys & Key West

Nautilimo

cruising in style

A happy-go-lucky wedding party celebrates the occasion on a Nautilimo sunset cruise with owner Joe Fox.

the trip

Tour the Keys in the world's first Cadillac-style, nautical stretch limousine! And like the Nautilimo itself, owner Joe Fox is a one-of-a-kind.

what to see

Joe built his Nautilimo by hand and here's how he did it: he created a 1987 Cadillac replica out of fiberglass and mounted it all on a boat. Then he added a custom Yamaha, four-stroke, 100-horsepower engine. Several accessory trips to the junkyard later and his dream had come true! Up to four people can take a short jaunt or a three-hour trip with music and champagne. It's available for birthdays, anniversaries, weddings or a romantic sunset cruise for two.

other highlights

This crazy contraption just makes everyone feel good! You will love the reaction from onlookers as Joe passes by waterfront restaurants and the like. By the way, Joe lives in a two-story houseboat once used in the 1960s television series *Surfside 6*, which he shares with his cat, "Mutiny" (He rescued her during Hurricane Hugo).

Matecumbe Marina
80500 Overseas Highway (U.S. 1)
Islamorada, FL 33060
(305) 517-9501

Admission: *One-hour tour: $90 for up to two passengers, $120 for three passengers, $140 for four passengers. Two-hour tour: $160 for up to two passengers, $210 for three passengers, $240 for four passengers. Three or more hours: Up to an additional $30 per person, per hour.*

Hours: *Tour times vary.*

www.nautilimo.com

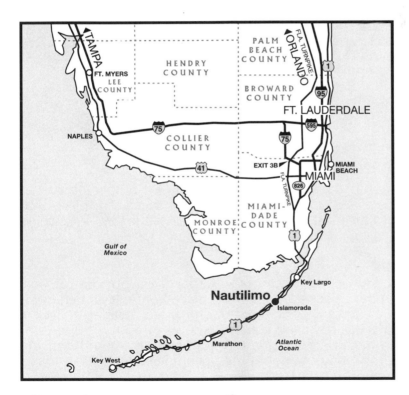

directions

From Tampa, take Interstate 75 to Exit 3B (Turnpike South) and merge onto the Florida Turnpike. Turn right onto South Dixie Highway which becomes U.S. 1 (Overseas Highway). Follow U.S. 1 about 40 miles to Matecumbe Marina where Nautilimo is docked.

"a Caddy for the Keys."

Robbie's of Islamorada

feed the tarpon!

Robbie's of Islamorada

Grab some bait fish and feed lunch to the schools of hungry tarpon who make Robbie's their home.

Robbie's of Islamorada

The Florida Keys & Key West

the trip

Here in the sportfishing capital of the world, we did not come to catch fish. Believe it or not, we came to feed them at a place that is certainly one of the most entertaining shows in all the Keys — Robbie's of Islamorada.

what to see

Robbie's is best known for "feeding the tarpon." For obvious reasons, these savvy fish have decided to call this place home. It all began 18 years ago with the feeding of an injured fish named "Scarface." Today, it's an amazing spectacle: hand-feeding schools of 50 to 100 tarpon. And when I say feed, I mean these big guys actually jump out of the water and take the food right out of your hand! For a few dollars and a bit of courage, you can do it too!

other highlights

You can't miss "Moss." He's the resident dog who treats pelicans like the sheep he was trained to herd. It's amazing to watch this little guy on patrol as he keeps pelicans from snatching bait fish that customers buy to feed the tarpon. Robbie's also offers offshore and reef fishing, as well as tours and boat rentals.

77522 Overseas Highway (U.S. 1) Islamorada, FL 33036
Toll free: (877) 664-8498
(305) 664-9814

Admission: *Fishing and tour rates vary.*
Tarpon feeding: $1, plus $2 for a pail of bait fish.

Hours: *Open daily 8 a.m. to 7 p.m.*

www.robbies.com

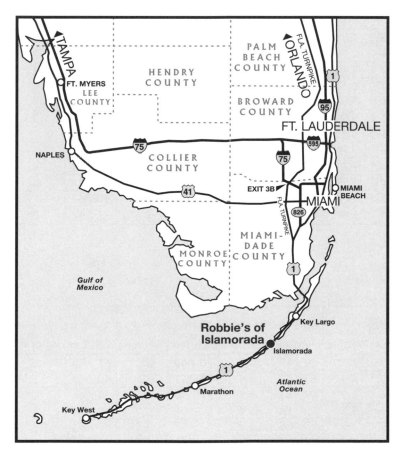

directions

From Tampa, take Interstate 75 to Exit 3B (Turnpike South) and merge onto the Florida Turnpike. Turn right onto South Dixie Highway which becomes U.S. 1 (Overseas Highway). Follow U.S. 1 about 40 miles to Robbie's of Islamorada.

Robbie's of Islamorada

"trust **me,** this **is** an absolutely **amazing** experience that **you'll** never forget."

weather guide

	Fort Myers		Jacksonville		Key West		Miami	
	High/Low	Rainfall	High/Low	Rainfall	High/Low	Rainfall	High/Low	Rainfall
January	74°/53°	1.8"	64°/42°	3.3"	75°/65°	2.0"	75°/59°	2.0"
February	76°/54°	2.2"	67°/44°	3.9"	75°/65°	1.8"	76°/60°	2.1"
March	80°/59°	3.1"	74°/50°	3.7"	79°/69°	1.7"	79°/64°	2.4"
April	85°/62°	1.1"	80°/56°	2.8"	82°/72°	1.8"	83°/68°	3.0"
May	89°/68°	3.9"	85°/63°	3.6"	85°/76°	3.5"	85°/72°	6.2"
June	91°/73°	9.5"	89°/70°	5.7"	88°/79°	5.1"	88°/75°	9.3"
July	91°/75°	8.3"	92°/73°	5.6"	89°/80°	3.6"	89°/77°	5.7"
August	91°/75°	9.7"	91°/72°	7.9"	89°/79°	5.0"	89°/77°	7.6"
September	90°/74°	7.8"	87°/70°	7.1"	88°/79°	5.9"	88°/76°	7.6"
October	86°/69°	2.9"	80°/60°	2.9"	84°/76°	4.4"	85°/72°	5.6"
November	81°/61°	1.6"	73°/50°	2.2"	80°/71°	2.8"	80°/67°	2.7"
December	76°/55°	1.6"	67°/44°	2.7"	76°/67°	2.0"	77°/62°	1.8"

	Orlando		Pensacola		Tampa Bay		Tallahassee	
	High/Low	Rainfall	High/Low	Rainfall	High/Low	Rainfall	High/Low	Rainfall
January	72°/51°	2.3"	60°/41°	4.7"	70°/49°	2.0"	63°/38°	4.8"
February	72°/50°	4.0"	63°/44°	5.4"	71°/51°	3.1"	66°/40°	5.5"
March	78°/56°	3.2"	69°/51°	5.7"	77°/56°	3.0"	73°/47°	6.2"
April	84°/61°	1.3"	76°/58°	3.4"	82°/61°	1.2"	80°/52°	3.7"
May	88°/67°	3.1"	83°/66°	4.2"	87°/67°	3.1"	86°/61°	4.8"
June	91°/72°	7.5"	89°/72°	6.4"	90°/73°	5.5"	91°/68°	6.9"
July	92°/74°	7.2"	90°/74°	7.4"	90°/74°	6.6"	91°/71°	8.8"
August	91°/74°	7.1"	89°/74°	7.3"	90°/74°	7.6"	91°/71°	7.5"
September	89°/73°	6.3"	86°/70°	5.4"	89°/73°	6.0"	88°/68°	5.6"
October	84°/67°	2.9"	79°/60°	4.1"	84°/65°	2.0"	81°/56°	2.9"
November	77°/57°	1.7"	70°/51°	3.5"	78°/57°	1.8"	73°/46°	3.9"
December	73°/52°	2.0"	63°/44°	4.3"	72°/52°	2.2"	66°/41°	5.0"

More One Tank Trips

about Florida weather

Heads Up, Readers!

As you make your plans to travel around Florida using *More* **One Tank Trips,** I thought you would like to know the average high and low temperatures, and rainfall, before heading out on the open road. For your convenience, I have prepared the accompanying chart for you to use as a reference.

For the most part, Florida weather is typically pleasant. In the summer, afternoon rains are almost a daily occurrence. But please be aware that there is always the possibility of dangerous lightning, tornadoes, floods and even hurricanes. Hurricane season begins in June and runs through the end of November. If you are in an area in which a hurricane is approaching, I urge you to take the news warnings seriously.

For the latest on weather in the Tampa Bay area, call us at **(813) 871-1313,** then press **"1."** Or log onto **www.wtvt.com**.

Here's wishing you lots of smiles and laughter and, above all, enjoy your travels!

Paul Dellegatto
WTVT FOX13 Chief Meteorologist

about Florida sports

Greeting Sports Fans!

As you look through the following list of sports attractions, you can see that those of us living in the Sunshine State take sports seriously. The listings are not just sports spots. They are also great destinations that many families, including my own, have enjoyed. After all, there is no greater excitement than a day at the ballpark, or an evening spent wildly cheering for the home team.

As Sports Director for **FOX13**, I can personally vouch for every venue on the following list of Sports Attractions. Our attraction list covers a wide range of sports within the state, from Major League Baseball to NASCAR.

So load up the family car and hit the road, and get ready to soak up some of our exhilarating Sunshine State Sports!

Chip Carter
WTVT FOX13 Sports Director

SUNSHINE STATE SPORTS ATTRACTIONS

Major League Baseball – www.majorleaguebaseball.com

Florida Marlins, Pro Player Stadium, Fort Lauderdale
Tampa Bay Devil Rays, Tropicana Field, St. Petersburg

Spring Training Exhibition Baseball (Grapefruit League)

Atlanta Braves, Disney's Wide World of Sports, Kissimmee
Baltimore Orioles, Fort Lauderdale Stadium, Fort Lauderdale
Boston Red Sox, City of Palms Park, Fort Myers
Cincinnati Reds, Ed Smith Stadium, Sarasota
Cleveland Indians, Chain of Lakes Park, Winter Haven
Detroit Tigers, Marchant Stadium, Lakeland
Florida Marlins, Space Coast Stadium, Viera-Melbourne

Houston Astros, Osceola County Stadium, Kissimmee
Kansas City Royals, Baseball City Stadium, Davenport
Los Angeles Dodgers, Dodgertown, Vero Beach
Montreal Expos, Municipal Stadium, West Palm Beach
New York Mets, St. Lucie County Stadium, Port St. Lucie
New York Yankees, Legends Field, Tampa
Philadelphia Phillies, Jack Russell Memorial Stadium, Clearwater
Pittsburgh Pirates, McKechnie Field, Bradenton
Tampa Bay Devil Rays, Florida Power Park, St. Petersburg
Texas Rangers, Charlotte County Stadium, Port Charlotte
Toronto Blue Jays, Dunedin Stadium, Dunedin

National Basketball Association – www.nba.com
Orlando Magic, Orlando Arena, Orlando
Miami Heat, American Airlines Arena, Miami

Women's National Basketball Association – www.wnba.com
Orlando Miracle, Orlando Arena, Orlando
Miami Sol, American Airlines Arena, Miami

National Football League – www.nfl.com
Tampa Bay Buccaneers, Raymond James Stadium, Tampa
Jacksonville Jaguars, Alltel Stadium, Jacksonville
Miami Dolphins, Pro Player Stadium, Fort Lauderdale

Arena Football League
Tampa Bay Storm, Ice Palace, Tampa
Orlando Predators, Orlando Arena, Orlando

National Hockey League – www.nhl.com
Tampa Bay Lightning, Ice Palace, Tampa
Florida Panthers, National Car Rental Center, Miami

Major League Soccer – www.mlsnet.com
Tampa Bay Mutiny, Raymond James Stadium, Tampa

NASCAR and International Racing – www.nascar.com
Daytona International Speedway, Daytona
Homestead-Miami Speedway, Homestead
Sebring International Raceway, Sebring
USA International Speedway, Lakeland

Division I College Athletics
Bethune-Cookman University, Daytona Beach
Florida A&M University, Tallahassee
Florida State University, Tallahassee
University of Central Florida, Orlando
University of Florida, Gainesville
University of Miami, Coral Gables
University of South Florida, Tampa

i n d e x

trip notes

A great way to travel is in your new Chrysler or Jeep. Visit your Chrysler and Jeep dealers today.

THERE'S ONLY ONE

Alan Jay Chrysler-Plymouth-Jeep 5330 U.S. 27 S., Sebring, FL 33870 (863) 382-1177

B.M. Smith Motors 1722 S. Collins St., Plant City, FL 33566 (813) 752-5167

Citrus Motors 12020 U.S. 301 Dade City, FL 33525 (352) 521-0055

Courtesy Chrysler-Jeep 1728 W. Brandon Blvd., Brandon, FL 33511 (813) 685-4511

Crystal Chrysler-Dodge-Jeep 1005 S. Suncoast Blvd., Homosassa, FL 34448 (352) 563-2277

Crystal Chrysler-Plymouth-Dodge-Jeep 2077 Hwy. 44 W., Inverness, FL 34450 (352) 726-1238

Dayton Andrews Chrysler-Plymouth-Jeep 2388 Gulf-to-Bay Blvd., Clearwater, FL 33765 (727) 799-4539

Ferman Chrysler-Plymouth-Jeep 1307 W. Kennedy Blvd., Tampa, FL 33606 (813) 253-2100

Ferman Chrysler-Plymouth-Jeep 11001 N. Florida Ave., Tampa, FL 33612 (813) 371-2600

Ferman Chrysler-Plymouth-Jeep of New Port Richey 3939 U.S. 19, New Port Richey, FL 34652 (727) 847-5555

Ferman of Wauchula 1401 U.S. 17 S., Wauchula, FL 33873 (863) 773-4744

Firkins Chrysler-Plymouth-Jeep 2700 First St., Bradenton, FL 34208 (941) 748-6510

Fitzgerald's Countryside Auto Mall 27365 U.S. 19 N., Clearwater, FL 33761 (727) 799-1800

Gettel Jeep of Sarasota 3480 Bee Ridge Road, Sarasota, FL 34239 (941) 923-1411

Lakeland Chrysler-Plymouth 2335 U.S. 98 N., Lakeland, FL 33805 (863) 687-2501

Nature Coast Chrysler Jeep 14358 Cortez Blvd., Brooksville, FL 34613 (352) 597-1265

Douglas Jeep 2382 S. Tamiami Trail, Venice, FL 34293 (941) 484-8300

Plaza Chrysler-Plymouth 14358 Cortez Blvd., Brooksville, FL 34613 (352) 597-1265

Regal Jeep 2615 Lakeland Hills Blvd., Lakeland, FL 33805 (863) 687-8000

Sarasota Chrysler-Plymouth 6826 S. Tamiami Trail, Sarasota, FL 34231 (941) 922-0711

St. Petersburg Chrysler-Plymouth-Jeep 2500 34th St. N., St. Petersburg, FL 33713 (727) 323-2000

Steve Sorensen Chrysler-Plymouth-Jeep 1900 U.S. 27 N., Lake Wales, FL 33853 (863) 676-0733

Suncoast Chrysler-Plymouth-Jeep 8755 Park Blvd., Seminole, FL 34642 (727) 393-4621

Tom Edwards 1425 W. Main St., Bartow, FL 33830 (863) 533-0793

Venice Chrysler-Plymouth 1550 S. Tamiami Trail, Venice, FL 34293 (941) 493-5204

Wells Motor Company 1600 U.S. 27 S., Avon Park, FL 33825 (863) 453-6644

Winter Haven Chrysler-Plymouth-Jeep 190 Avenue "K" S.W., Winter Haven, FL 33880 (863) 299-1243